From Bell

Oct., 16 - 1959

Bertha A. Palmer.

First Church of the Brethren
1340 Forge Road
Carlisle, Pennsylvania 17013

PATHS

OF

SHINING

LIGHT

PATHS OF SHINING LIGHT

Vera Idol

ABINGDON PRESS
New York • Nashville

PATHS OF SHINING LIGHT

Copyright © MCMLVI by Pierce & Washabaugh

Library of Congress Catalog Card Number: 56-6355

SET UP, PRINTED, AND BOUND BY THE
PARTHENON PRESS, AT NASHVILLE,
TENNESSEE, UNITED STATES OF AMERICA

Dedicated to

MY SISTER

VERTA IDOL COE

With Love

Foreword

✤✤✤

The idea for this book originated mainly in three areas of my life. The most immediate impetus came from three morning devotions which I conducted for a group of college students in beautiful little Lindley Chapel of High Point College.

For several years the various religious organizations on the campus have held brief daily devotions six mornings each week of the college year, three of which are led by faculty members. Last fall I chose as topics for my meetings Mountains, Valleys, and Trees as inspirations to the worship of God. Subsequently several students asked for copies of the talks; so the desire grew in my heart to add to these subjects other great elements in God's world, and thereby create a book of worship programs based on nature. Since I am a teacher of literature and for many years taught a Sunday-school class of young women, I have sought to enrich and magnify my own thoughts by illustrations and quotations from the Bible and other great works of literature that my students and I have studied together.

Though chronologically it came first, the second impelling motive was unforgettable days which my sister and I spent with our treasured friend, Mabel Cherry, returned missionary from Korea and Bible teacher in our city schools, at her lovely cottage at Lake Junaluska, North Carolina. Each morning, after a pleasant, leisurely breakfast, we sat for an hour on the front porch of the cottage facing the beautiful lake and the white cross—high on a mountain peak across the lake—which is the symbol of the religious purpose to which Lake Junaluska is dedicated. Behind the cross other mountain peaks rose till they were lost in the hazy sky. It was a wonderful hour. One of us would read aloud from the Bible or another inspirational book of worship, then there would be

7

a quiet prayer, or silent minutes of meditation. I shall never forget those hours, withdrawn as we were from the noisy, restless world, hearing only the occasional song of a bird, and surrounded by the majesty and beauty of God's everlasting hills. Many of the thoughts in this book were born during those quiet hours.

The third source goes farther back to sights and sounds that through the years have grown into my being from many vacations spent among mountains and beside the sea; from fortunate glimpses of beautiful spots in faraway places that will remain in my memory; and from the inestimable privilege I have had of increasing my own joy in such beauty by entering, even though humbly and imperfectly, into the "best and happiest moments" of some "of the happiest and best minds" of today and other days. For all these sources of inspiration I give grateful thanks.

I wish to express my particular thanks to Miss Thelma Patrick of High Point for continued encouragement and support in this undertaking; to Miss Marcella Carter, librarian of High Point College, for helpful criticism and invaluable assistance in seeking sources for copyright permissions; to Miss Clarice Bowman, professor of religion at High Point College, for helpful advice and suggestions; and to my sister, Verta Idol Coe, and her daughters, Julia and Mary Ann, for inspiration and encouragement.

My grateful thanks to Faye Peedin, a fine student of High Point College, and member of the class of 1956, for careful typing of my manuscript, and for devoting hours to work with me on the mechanical end of the book.

I give my sincere thanks for the prompt and cheerful co-operation given by those who hold copyrights on the many passages quoted in this book.

VERA IDOL

Contents

"O heavenly Father, who hast filled the world with beauty; Open, we beseech thee, our eyes to behold thy gracious hand in all thy works; that rejoicing in thy whole creation, we may learn to serve thee with gladness."

—BOOK OF COMMON PRAYER

Chapter 1

ROADS

❖❖❖

"Prepare ye the way of the Lord, make straight in the desert a highway for our God. . . . : and the crooked shall be made straight, and the rough places plain."

—Isa. 40:3, 4

"But the path of the just is as the shining light, that shineth more and more unto the perfect day."

—Prov. 4:18

High on a mountain in western North Carolina is a point to which the feet of thousands of visitors have beaten a worn path. Far below in the valley a lone cabin stands in complete isolation. The narrow road leading to it—the only means of access—is now no more than the trace of a grass-grown trail losing itself in the trees and undergrowth on the mountain sides. It does not appear to have ever been more than a trail, able to be used only by a man on foot or on horseback. One wonders how people could ever have existed in a spot so withdrawn and inaccessible; yet old-time natives of the area tell the story of a man and woman who lived their entire married lives in that cabin in the valley, rearing a large family of sons and daughters to adulthood. The cabin is deserted now; the father and mother are dead; and the children have found roads leading to many parts of the world, where some of them have become well known, and all of them are leading lives of service and usefulness. That weed-choked trail, now all but obliterated, once brought to the sequestered family those necessities for living which could not be provided on the tiny farm surrounding the cabin. One by one the children followed this path to the outside world on the mountaintop, where there were schools to teach them of the world of books, and a world of people to teach them the art of getting along with others. Here there were opportunities to build their lives toward definite aims and plans.

Most roads, however, are not so hidden. They are built to lead somewhere, to pass certain spots, to make areas accessible, and to give dwellers an outlet to the rest of the world. Roads show stages of development, just as other phases of civilization. It is a far cry from the narrow lanes, generally impassable during much of the year because of deep muddy ruts, to the broad intricate superhighways with roadbeds as smooth as the floors in our homes. A large part of the traffic of the world passes along the broad highways that penetrate the farthest reaches of the civilized lands. Much of the food that feeds the hungry world reaches its destination by highways. Many necessities and luxuries, as well as books to feed the minds and souls of men, pass over these roads. Men and women travel the highways to follow every pursuit of their lives: gaining an education, earning a livelihood, seeking pleasure and enjoyment, and serving God and their fellow men. There is another, and sadder, side to the picture: in this day of speed, carelessness, and too little regard for the safety of ourselves or others, death often stalks the highways. Christ's words, "Broad is the way that leadeth to destruction," have become literally and tragically true.

Roads have had a great part to play in Christianizing the world. One of the things a missionary must do as he begins his work in a remote region of an untraveled country is to open trails to enable him to establish contact with those he has come to serve. Then, as hospitals, schools, and churches rise in the compounds and begin spreading their mission of healing the bodies, teaching the minds, and saving the souls of the natives, the trails must be widened to make the way easier. Then do the words of Isaiah come true: "Prepare ye the way of the Lord, make straight in the desert a highway for our God."

There may be roads leading to all the good places in the world, but because of our carelessness, wickedness, or often sheer indifference, we do not always make our way to places where the fine things of life are found. Sometimes we lose our way or pass by the fine things of life, and occasionally we do not want to find them. And then, we may find ourselves in places where we never intended to go. We are too much like

14

Alice in the rabbit hole. You remember that Alice said to the Cheshire Cat, "Would you tell me, please, which way I ought to go from here?"

"That depends a good deal on where you want to get to," was the Cat's reply.

Then Alice said, "I don't much care where—"

And the Cat continued, "Then it doesn't matter which way you go."

To have a definite goal and the right objective is the fundamental basis of a successful life. Our success or failure depends on the road we select and how hard we try to keep faithfully on the right road. We need to pray with the psalmist, "Teach me thy way, O Lord, and lead me in a plain path" (27:11). And as we rely on God to guide us, we repeat, "Thou wilt show me the path of life."

Robert Frost, beloved American poet, once wrote:

> I shall be telling this with a sigh
> Somewhere ages and ages hence:
> Two roads diverged in a wood, and I—
> I took the one less travelled by,
> And that has made all the difference.[1]

Yes, it makes all the difference which road we follow as we go through life. Roads may guide us to schools or churches; to halls where we hear great music, or to galleries where we may see wonderful works of art; or they may lead to lowest places of sin and vice, away from all that is lovely, fine, and good. The choice is ours. The true test of a man's character is the way that leads him to happiness. To one who finds his happiness following in the footsteps of the Master, all his ways are pleasant and his paths lead only to peace. Jesus spoke of himself as the "Light of the World." He is the Light that shows us the road ahead, that prevents us from stumbling in the dark or losing our way. Let us follow the roads that lead to the lofty mountaintops, through the peaceful valleys, and along the still-running rivers. The roads we choose can lead us into all the beautiful works of creation, where "God may be had for the asking," and we shall find that: "The path of the just is as the shining light, that shineth more and more unto the perfect day" (Prov. 4:18).

[1] "The Road Not Taken," from *Complete Poems of Robert Frost*. Copyright 1930, 1949 by Henry Holt and Company, Inc. Copyright 1936, 1948 by Robert Frost. By permission of the publishers.

Chapter II

MOUNTAINS

❖❖

> "He stood, and measured the earth: he beheld, and drove asunder the nations; and the everlasting mountains were scattered, the perpetual hills did bow: his ways are everlasting."
>
> *—Hab. 3:6*

> "I will lift up mine eyes unto the hills, from whence cometh my help."
>
> *—Ps. 121:1*

From time immemorial many people in all lands have found inspiration and help from the great hills that rise toward the sky and spread outward until their silhouettes are lost in the misty clouds on the horizon.

Repeatedly through the Bible great events took place on mountain peaks. It was on Mount Sinai, where the glory of God abode as a cloud for six days, that Moses met God face to face, in the midst of clouds, thunder, and lightning, and received his commandments. It was to the top of Pisgah in the mountains of Nebo that God called Moses to view the "Promised Land." Here occurred the climax of Moses' tragedy. Because of disobedience to one of God's commands, he was not able to enter the land, but only to look upon it from afar, although he had led the chosen people through trials and hardships to the very gateway of their destination. How often this tragedy is repeated in many of our lives. We are guilty of disobedience and other sins that close the doors of fulfillment to many dreams and aspirations that might have been attained if we had remained true to God. The blessed compensation is that if we turn to God with our whole hearts, he opens doors to other opportunities. Moses died on lofty Nebo, and no one knows where he

17

was buried, but he will live forever as the great leader, lawgiver, and guide of the children of Israel through the wilderness.

Many other mountain peaks in the Old and New Testaments are closely associated with Bible experiences. Mount Zion is always a symbol of the New Jerusalem. The temple in Jerusalem, heart and hope of Israel, was built upon a hill; Jerusalem itself was a city set upon hills. Hear the voices of exiles returning to the Holy City from afar as they catch the first sight of the foothills surrounding the beloved city, and burst into an exultant cry, "I will lift up mine eyes unto the hills, from whence cometh my help" (Ps. 121:1).

The hills around the Sea of Galilee were intimately related to the earthly ministry of Jesus. At difficult periods in his ministry and before events of special significance, such as the selection of his disciples, he withdrew into the mountains to pray, often remaining all night in prayer. Much of his teaching was done as he sat among his followers on a hillside. Many of his greatest teachings are included in the "Sermon on the Mount." The most distinctive experience of Peter, James, and John occurred when they were permitted to share with Jesus his exaltation on the Mount of Transfiguration, and to hear with their own ears the voice of God himself proclaim, "This is my beloved Son: hear him." The terrible, tragic last hours of Christ's life on earth—the ultimate in his love for humanity—were spent on Mount Olivet, the hill of Calvary, near the city of Jerusalem.

The association of these sacred events, and many others, must cause serious, thoughtful people to look reverently upon lofty mountain ranges. It must give to any nature lover an appreciation of their majestic beauty; for such beauty is not to be found in any other manifestation of nature.

Can we stand on any lofty peak and gaze far into the distance, seeing the mighty hills piled one on another, stretching on until their misty outlines blend with the sky itself, and not be reminded of the infinity of God? His mercy and kindness are as boundless as the mountains. Do we not see in the everlastingness of the mountains the ceaseless goodness of God? They stand, changeless through the years, yet changing with each hour of the day, from one season to the next, and with every change of atmospheric conditions. So does the steadfastness of God's love reach down into the constantly changing circumstances of our lives to suit his blessings to our individual and changing needs.

At times we wake in the morning among the mountains to find ourselves closed in by an impenetrable fog which shuts out even the faintest outline of the hills. However, even as we look, shadowy shapes begin to appear, and almost before we are aware of it, the mist has dissolved, and the mountains stand revealed in pure sunlight against the azure of a clear sky. It is often thus in our lives. We find ourselves shut in by clouds of doubt, mists of unhappiness or sorrow, and feel as if God has withdrawn himself from us. Our soul's vision is often more limited than our physical sight, and we cry out against the enclosing mists. But God is more surely there all the time than are the mountain peaks behind the fog, and if we wait, the sunshine of his love will bring back to us the beauty, the peace, and the serenity, that seemed for a time withdrawn.

The mountains reflect many other of God's qualities. Lofty peaks rising to the sky, or towering snow-covered and losing themselves above the clouds are symbols of mighty and everlasting strength. As they stand unmoved when storm clouds pour their torrents on their slopes and winds tear at them and roar through their passes, we are thus reminded of the strength and enduring quality of God's love and care for us. In the evening when the glory of the setting sun still lights the tallest peaks and the distant hills are purpled by lengthening shadows, our hearts become quiet and serene, soothed by the "peace that passeth understanding." We seem to hear God saying, "Be still, and know that I am God."

Truly, we can see God's glory reflected in his handiwork among the mighty hills. If we open our hearts to God among his mountains, they can become to us symbols of all the great emotions of Christian living: beauty, strength, hope, serenity, faith, and the comfort of God's everlasting presence in the world.

Chapter III

VALLEYS

❖◆❖

> "Every valley shall be exalted, and
> every mountain and hill shall be made
> low; and the crooked shall be made
> straight, and the rough places plain:
> And the glory of the Lord shall be re-
> vealed, and all flesh shall see it together:
> for the mouth of the Lord hath spoken
> it." —*Isa. 40:4-5*

> "And I will give her her vineyards
> from thence, and the valley of Achor
> for a door of hope." —*Hos. 2:15*

In simple words which give a picture of natural scenery and symbolize an experience of life, someone once said, "Never a high hill, but there is some valley near."

The valley may be a gorge, deep ravine, or a canyon; it may be only wide enough to contain a small village; or it may extend for miles with great cities sprawling over its length and breadth. In the past cities were built on hills in order that the mountains might serve as fortresses against rude and savage invaders. Men occasionally build their homes on windswept mountains, and many small cabins cling so precariously to the hillsides that they seem almost inaccessible. But most great cities have flourished in the wide valleys; and in the smaller mountain coves nestle many tiny villages where people pursue their everyday ways of life, undisturbed by the changing tides of affairs in the greater world outside. I have often stood on scenic "lookouts" in the North Carolina mountains, and watched smoke rising from chimneys below, mute evidence of human life, and rather envied the quiet, simple life of the people there. One sees a church spire rising above the other roofs, and identifies a school-house by the children playing around it. Sometimes smokestacks that

21

belch dirty smoke and soil the cleanness and freshness of the atmosphere rise above industrial plants. But all of this is life—work and play, study and worship, life and death—the picture of life in its entirety.

The valleys are generally fertile spots. The soil is enriched by earth and minerals washed down the mountainsides, and by deposits left by streams as they cut their way through the valleys. Rain from the clouds and mists that form along the valleys water the land and make it rich and fertile. The psalmist gave us a wonderful picture of the richness of the valley when he said, "The pastures are clothed with flocks; the valleys also are covered over with corn; they shout for joy; they also sing" (Ps. 65:13).

To bring forth fruit from the earth is to fulfill one of God's earliest commands; feeding a hungry and starving people is one of the basic missionary contributions. People whose physical bodies are suffering from malnutrition and starvation cannot be expected to take much interest in having their souls fed with spiritual food. So from the rich valleys of Christian lands, food must be sent to foreign lands; and ignorant people must be instructed in ways to raise their own crops and produce their own food as they learn the lessons of Christian living.

A towering mountain rises proudly above its surroundings; a valley lies humbly at its foot. True humility is an essential virtue. No individual can grow and develop to his full stature who does not face life with a certain pride born of self-confidence, but with humility in the face of all that he does not know. "Blessed are the meek: for they shall inherit the earth" is not a command, but the statement of an eternal truth. Only the teachable and those who are willing to humble themselves before goodness and greatness have the capability of inheriting the riches of the world of learning.

Peace of mind is one of the most widely-sought attributes in the world today. Many volumes have been published and thousands of sermons preached on how to attain peace. Where in all the world of nature can we find a more nearly perfect setting for peace than in a beautiful valley as it catches the glory of the morning sunrise, the quiet of the lengthening evening shadows, and the stillness of starlight or moonlight? Robert Service, Alaskan poet of the Yukon, wrote:

> I've stood in some mighty-mouthed hollow
> That's plumb full of hush to the brim;

I've watched the big, husky sun wallow
In crimson and gold, and grow dim,
Till the moon set the pearly peaks gleaming,
And the stars tumbled out, neck and crop;
And I've thought that I surely was dreaming,
With the peace o' the world piled on top.[1]

Since figuratively speaking, most of the people live in the valleys, it is there that most of our Christian work must be done. Moses abode with God on Mount Sinai for forty days and forty nights, listening as God instructed him in the laws which should guide his chosen people; but the time came when Moses left the Mount and went down into the valley to teach the people what God had taught him. There he found that during his long absence, the people had melted their gold into the image of a golden calf, and were engaging in the same abominable rites which their heathen neighbors practiced. Moses' anger against the people was great, and he turned again to God for instructions. God sent him back to his task of leading the people through the desert; of slowly with great long-suffering showing them the evils of their ways, and turning them back to God. Suppose Moses had refused to serve in the valley? Peter, James, and John, after the glory of the vision on the Mount of Transfiguration, longed to remain and proposed to build a temple there, but God sent them back to the valley. There they found sick, suffering, and needy people to whom they must minister.

It is tremendously important that man should catch the glory and meaning of God on the mountaintop; but unless he can carry that glory into the lives of others in the valleys, the vision will fade into nothingness. We can save our lives only by losing them in service to our fellow men. Unless we use our talents we shall lose them, as did the unfaithful steward who buried his one talent in the ground. Anything that is not used becomes useless. A beautiful unused voice loses its power. A great pianist is quoted as having said that if he failed to practice one day, he knew it; if he missed a week, his audiences knew it. Service is the keynote of Christianity. On the mountain peaks we see God in his glory and catch the vision of his might and power; it is in the valley that we translate the power into service to our fellow men.

[1] "The Spell of the Yukon," used by permission of the publishers, Dodd, Mead & Co., Inc., New York and The Ryerson Press, Toronto, Canada.

Chapter IV

OCEANS

❖❖

> "And God said, Let the waters under the heaven be gathered together unto one place, and let the dry land appear: and it was so. And God called the dry land Earth; and the gathering together of the waters called he Seas: and God saw that it was good."
>
> —*Gen. 1:9-10*

> "And, behold, there arose a great tempest in the sea, insomuch that the ship was covered with the waves: but he was asleep. And his disciples came to him, and awoke him, saying, Lord, save us; we perish. And he saith unto them, Why are ye fearful, O ye of little faith? Then he arose, and rebuked the winds and the sea; and there was a great calm."
>
> —*Matt. 8:24-26*

W*e* sing in our churches the familiar hymn:

> There's a wideness in God's mercy,
> Like the wideness of the sea.

The full meaning of these words cannot be felt until one has stood on the deck of a ship in the middle of the ocean, far from any sign of land, seeing nothing but wide wastes of water as far as eye can reach. Until he has seen it thus, it is hard for him to imagine the immensity of the oceans that divide continent from continent. Although the experience of the biblical writers was limited mainly to sailing on inland seas and sometimes on the "Great Sea," they wrote feelingly of the width and depth of the great waters. What would they have said if they had lived until all the seas had been discovered and the globe circumnavigated? How distance widened as new lands were discovered, and men traveled weeks and even months in sailboats from country to country! Then, how the distance narrowed as faster-than-sound airplanes crossed oceans in a fraction of the time formerly required!

When the psalmist wrote that God planned for man to have dominion over everything in the world, little did he dream of the meaning of his words. We do not yet know the full extent of man's dominion, if he will only use the power God has put into his hands for beneficent inventions instead of horrible machines to destroy mankind. Let us never attribute to God the misuse of knowledge; God made us free to choose good or evil. In the wideness of his mercy there seems to be no limit to what man may achieve; let us pray with our whole hearts for men of good will who will use their knowledge to bring peace on earth.

There is no greater evidence of the power of God than in the might of the sea. How puny are the works of man when stormy seas beat upon them! Men build great ships that can sometimes survive terrible storms; but at other times an angry sea can break such a boat to pieces like a child's toy. Houses of brick and stone crumble like clay in the path of the hurricane; and even the very sands of the shore where they stood are washed back into the sea whence they came. In the midst of grief caused by such cataclysms, we stand awed in the presence of God and exclaim with the psalmist, "Thy path in the great waters, and thy footsteps are not known" (11:19), or again, "The Lord on high is mightier than the noise of many waters, yea, than the mighty waves of the sea" (93:4).

Just as the sea is awful in its wrath, so it is beatific in its peace—one of God's contrasts. We may sail for days over sparkling, sun-kissed waters, broken only by the white crests of tiny wavelets. We may sit on a sandy beach for hours watching lazy breakers roll in so slowly and gently that tiny children laugh and play in them with no fear or danger. The greatest picture of peace after a storm and God's power over nature is the story of the fearful disciples caught in a great tempest on the Sea of Galilee. Christ was asleep. When he was awakened he questioned the disciples concerning their lack of faith; nevertheless he rebuked the wind and waves. And the story ends with simple, powerful words: "And there was a great calm."

There are those who say that the ocean is tiring to them because of its monotony. How can anyone think thus? It is never the same, from hour to hour, day to day, or from season to season. We exclaim that the sea is as blue as sapphire; before we finish speaking, it may be emerald or turquoise, or clouds may cover the sky, and the water turn a murky gray. The water one day may be as smooth as a millpond, and the very next day be whipped into mountain-high waves. Byron may be inspired to cry, "Roll on, thou deep and dark blue ocean, roll!" Or Coleridge may see a picture of calm,

> As idle as a painted ship
> Upon a painted ocean.

Whatever its mood, there is always beauty. Such beauty as can come only from the heart of the Creator to delight his children whom he has imbued with love and appreciation for the beautiful things he made for them.

To one who lives beside the ocean, love for the water is like the love of a man for his sweetheart. No matter how far away he may go or how long he may stay, his heart still goes back; and he never misses an opportunity for a visit, short or long, to a spot where he can see, hear, and smell the ocean. The sea is so close to all of England that love for it is part of an Englishman's heritage. Therefore it is not strange that English poetry is filled with love for the sea. From the earliest Anglo-Saxon writers to the most modern, it would hardly be possible to mention any poet who has omitted some allusions to the ocean. Perhaps the most moving poem concerning the sea is John Masefield's "Sea-Fever." John Masefield went to sea as a young lad, and during those impressionable years, he sailed in many kinds of ships over a large number of the seas of the world. He makes us feel with him a great homesickness for the wild, free life on the open sea in this stanza from the poem:

> I must go down to the seas again, for the call of the running tide
> Is a wild call and a clear that may not be denied;
> And all I ask is a windy day with the white clouds flying,
> And the flung spray and the blown spume, and the sea-gulls crying.[1]

The "stern and rock-bound coast" of New England, the "dashing waves" of the North Atlantic, were closely woven into the fabric of

---

[1] Used by permission of the publishers, The Macmillan Co.

Whittier's life. This poet found the basis of his simple faith in the life of Jesus as the Saviour carried on his ministry "beside the Syrian Sea." Whittier's love for Christ and his faith in him were beautiful and childlike. With complete confidence in the promises of God, he experienced no fear during a long life guided by the "inner light" of the Quaker faith. In "The Eternal Goodness" he uses the ocean as a symbol of his reliance on God for care and protection:

> And so beside the Silent Sea
> I wait the muffled oar;
> No harm from Him can come to me
> On ocean or on shore.
>
> I know not where His islands lift
> Their fronded palms in air;
> I only know I cannot drift
> Beyond His love and care.

No element in nature is fuller of mystery than the ocean. As we look across the ocean, and realize that it stretches far beyond our ability to see, until its waves wash another shore thousands of miles away; that mountains are submerged in its depth, and that in many places it reaches immeasurable depth, it takes our breath away. Its vastness is beyond human comprehension. Another thought assails us—what infinite Power prevents that vast body of water from sweeping with all its force across the land to join another ocean on the other side of the continent? Then the words of Jeremiah come to us and we bow in great humility and awe before the majesty of God:

"Fear ye not me? saith the Lord: will ye not tremble at my presence, which have placed the sand for the bound of the sea by a perpetual decree, that it cannot pass it: and though the waves thereof toss themselves, yet can they not prevail; though they roar, yet can they not pass over it?" (5:22).

When we hear of the life that goes on in the depths of its waters, we are left agape and confounded. There are huge creatures, and those so small as to be almost microscopic; some so dangerous that even other sea creatures fear them, and others so harmless we can hold them in our hands; ugly, ungainly monsters, and delicate, fairylike fish of every imaginable hue. There they all are, hidden and living their span of life in and under that great, restless, heaving mass of water!

What a mystery is the ebb and flow of the tides. With clocklike regularity, quietly and almost imperceptibly, the tide comes in until it has reached its height, and then with a rhythm as strange, it sweeps out to sea again. Thus it has happened, twice daily, era after era, since the dawn of time, and will be still ebbing and flowing with the same precision, ages after the world has forgotten that we ever lived. How great is God who can set in motion and maintain such perfection of rhythm as that! No other poet has been able to put into words the whole picture of the sea as Sidney Lanier has done in "The Marshes of Glynn." One should read the whole poem to catch its reverent comprehension and full meaning, but a few lines can suggest the magnitude of his understanding: "Oh, what is abroad in the marsh and the terminal sea?" he asks; and later with almost childlike wistfulness:

And I would I could know what swimmeth below when the tide comes in
On the length and the breadth of the marvelous marshes of Glynn.

No one has surpassed Lanier in the expression of complete trust and confidence in God as set forth in this stanza from the same poem:

> As the marsh-hen secretly builds on the watery sod,
> Behold I will build me a nest on the greatness of God:
> I will fly in the greatness of God as the marsh-hen flies
> In the freedom that fills all the space twixt the marsh and the skies:
> By so many roots as the marsh-grass sends in the sod
> I will heartily lay me a-hold on the greatness of God:
> Oh, like to the greatness of God is the greatness within
> The range of the marshes, the liberal marshes of Glynn.

As we think about the ocean, its might, mystery, and vastness, the only words that can express our feelings are those of the psalmist:

O Lord, how manifold are thy works! in wisdom hast thou made them all: the earth is full of thy riches.

So is this great and wide sea, wherein are things creeping innumerable, both small and great beasts.

There go the ships: there is that leviathan, whom thou hast made to play therein. (104:24-26.)

Ewing Galloway

Chapter V

STARS

>❖❖❖<

"There shall come a Star out of Jacob, and a Sceptre shall rise out of Israel."

—Num. 24:17

"Where is he that is born King of the Jews? for we have seen his Star in the east, and are come to worship him."

—Matt. 2:2

"There is one glory of the sun, and another glory of the moon, and another glory of the stars: for one star differeth from another star in glory."

—I Cor. 15:41

We have slight knowledge of astronomy to teach us even a little about the infinity of space, the many solar systems that fill the endless reaches of the firmament, and the unnumbered millions of stars that shine in skies that stretch beyond the most fantastic imagination of man. Although scientifically we know nothing of all these things, to stand out-of-doors on a cloudless, starlit night, gazing up into the indescribable beauty of the heavens makes us think with awe and reverence, "O Lord our Lord, how excellent is thy name in all the earth! Who hath set thy glory above the heavens" (Ps. 8:1). And in our hearts echo the words of Paul to the Corinthians: "There is one glory of the sun, and another glory of the moon, and another glory of the stars: for one star differeth from another star in glory" (I Cor. 5:41).

Travelers to all parts of the world bring home stories of the difference in the pageant of the stars in various places and at different seasons of

31

the year; yet each story is an attempt to put into words the glory of the stars, and to express the emotion of the traveler as he looks into a sky studded with twinkling and shining points of light. Our inability to comprehend fully these works of God makes us consider anew the power of a Creator who not only filled space—however you define space —with heavenly bodies, but controls and orders their "going up and their coming down," with such precision and system that the whole universe moves with absolute perfection. In our humble adoration we are led to cry:

When I consider thy heavens, the work of thy fingers, the moon and the stars, which thou hast ordained;
What is man, that thou art mindful of him? and the son of man, that thou visiteth him? (Ps. 8:3.)

Yet we, as Christians, can look up to the Creator of such incomprehensible magnitude, and like trusting children, call him Father, and take to him our smallest problems, knowing that his ear is ever open to even the humblest of his followers.

Perhaps the very loftiness of the position of the stars and their unattainability have made them symbols of inspiration. Emerson said, "Hitch your wagon to a star." An ideal must always remain beyond our reach. When we attain it, it ceases to be an ideal. The "gleam" must always lead onward and upward. So Christ is the perfect ideal. The more Christlike a Christian becomes, the more he realizes that in this life he can never hope to live the full life which Christ lived before him.

For long years and many generations the Hebrew people had waited and looked for the promised Messiah. The prophets had foretold his coming, but the hope in many hearts grew faint as the years went by and the promise was not fulfilled. In the early days the prophet had written, "There shall come a Star out of Jacob"; and the faith in loyal hearts, though often weak and all but extinguished, burned on, until at last it burst forth in the surpassing brilliance of the star that led wise men to Bethlehem, and then stood still above the manger which cradled the Infant Jesus. There, according to promise, the Saviour of the world was born; one who was to be called Wonderful Counselor, Mighty God, the Prince of Peace, and whose name would be Jesus; for he should save his people from their sins.

Thus, the star of Bethlehem is a vital part of our celebration of Christmas everywhere. Stars decorate our homes and churches, and crown Christmas trees from the huge ones in city squares to the tiny ones in the humblest homes. Repeatedly we read and recite the words of the wise men, "We have seen his star in the east and are come to worship him" (Matt. 2:2). And just as long ago the wise men left everything to come and worship him, so today if the world is to be saved, all men must find their way by that same star to kneel and worship the Christ. His way alone can lead men from godlessness, greed, and lust for power to salvation. The very existence of life in the world can continue and the world itself be saved only by turning to him and following his way of life.

In a world where sorrow and suffering abound, stars have stood for hope and consolation to sad hearts. Emerson once said, "There's no rood has not a star above it." To see the star is the true test of a Christian; too many of us are prone to fasten our eyes on the "rood" and not lift them high enough to see the star. The lines of Whittier, the good Quaker poet, who wrote so often with a quiet, unquestioning faith, have comforted many people:

> Alas for him who never sees
> The stars shine through his cypress-trees!
> Who, hopeless, lays his dead away,
> Nor looks to see the breaking day
> Across the mournful marbles play!
> Who hath not learned in hours of faith,
> The truth to flesh and sense unknown,
> That Life is ever lord of Death,
> And Love can never lose its own!

In keeping with the steadfast faith which he attained after struggling with doubts for years, Tennyson's last poem, written when he was eighty, breathes such calm faith and serene acceptance of death, that it has become one of the most beloved poems in the world, and is known by half of the English-speaking world:

> Sunset and evening star,
> And one clear call for me!
> And may there be no moaning of the bar
> When I put out to sea.

33

In early days all navigation was directed by the stars. "Constant as the north star" became proverbial. Shakespeare wrote:

> But I am constant as the northern star,
> Of whose true-fix'd and resting quality
> There is no fellow in the firmament.[1]

It is the happy privilege of most of us to know a few Christians whose faith in God is so firm and constant that their very lives breathe a sweetness and serenity which blesses all who come near them. Of them it can be truly said, "Their faith is constant as the northern star."

Matthew Arnold taught by his father, the famous headmaster of Rugby, to question and prove all things, learned his lesson so well that for a long time doubt governed his life. His poetry was full of unanswered questions; until at last, largely through the ministration of nature, his faith in God became steadfast. One of the greatest object lessons he received was from the quiet work of the stars—

> Still do thy sleepless ministers move on,
> Their glorious tasks in silence perfecting.

Just as they tranquilly perform their appointed work, undisturbed by the feverish restlessness and selfishness in the world below, so can man accomplish his mission in life as God ordained. His conviction of the satisfaction attained is expressed in two of the loveliest lines in poetry:

> For with joy the stars perform their shining,
> And the sea its long moon-silvered roll.

Have all of us on some late afternoon not been thrilled, as we saw the evening star shining brightly in the afterglow of a clear sunset low in the western sky? The truth of Wordsworth's lines came upon us:

> Fair as a star, when only one
> Is shining in the sky.

And what peace and rest are suggested by the two lines from Thomas Campbell:

> Star that bringest home the bee,
> And sett'st the weary labourer free!

[1] *Julius Caesar*, Act III, scene 1.

Thank God for our homes and for the evening star that leads us there.

The star has been accepted as the symbol of noteworthy achievements. Wordsworth wrote of Milton, "Thy soul was like a star, and dwelt apart," and the world has paid homage to the great epics of that starlike soul. One of the most matchless tributes to Lincoln is "When Lilacs Last in Dooryard Bloom'd" by Walt Whitman. In this elegy Whitman paid homage to Lincoln in three suitable symbols: a spray of white lilacs, homely flower blooming in yards the nation over; the clear, haunting note of a secluded hermit thrush; and the setting evening star. John, near the close of his life, in his book of Revelation, wrote of Christ: "I am the root and the offspring of David, and the bright and morning star" (Rev. 22:16). So we, like the "star-led wizards" of old, can find in the stars a guide, a hope, a consolation, and the Son of God himself.

Chapter VI

RIVERS

❖❖

> "He cutteth out rivers among the rocks; and his eye seeth every precious thing."
>
> *—Job 28:10*

> "And he shewed me a pure river of water of life, clear as crystal, proceeding out of the throne of God and of the Lamb."
>
> *—Rev. 22:1*

Water covers three fourths of the earth's surface and constitutes a large percentage of the elements that make up all vegetable and animal matter. No life could exist without water. In the beginning, according to Genesis, the earth was covered with water. Before there was light, "darkness was upon the face of the deep. And the Spirit of God moved upon the face of the waters" (1:2). On the second day God used the dry land to separate one body of water from another.

When God created Adam and Eve, he placed them in a rich garden in a fertile valley, but much of the country in which the Bible scenes were laid was desert or semidesert. The streams that were full and ran rapidly in the rainy season became slow, muddy threads, or dried up altogether during the dry season. People settled near the springs that existed here and there over the desert, or dug wells before raising tents for a camp. Because of the scarcity of water, famines were common in the land. When such a famine struck the land where Isaac was dwelling, the Lord appeared to him and sent him into the valley of Gerar where his father Abraham had abode and had dug wells. The hostile Philistines had filled up the wells, knowing that the lack of water would drive Abraham, his followers, and cattle away. Isaac dug them anew, and also found other wells of springing water, around which the ancestral seat of the twelve leaders of the tribes of Israel was established.

Throughout the Bible recur stories of the importance of water, as well as hundreds of figurative allusions to its significance in the natural or spiritual life of the people. The knowledge of God is likened to water in a thirsty land. Christ said to the woman at the well:

"Whosoever drinketh of this water shall thirst again: But whosoever drinketh of the water that I shall give him shall never thirst; but the water that I shall give him shall be in him a well of water springing up into everlasting life." (John 4:13-14.) David said, "He leadeth me beside the still waters," and Isaiah cried, "Ho, every one that thirsteth, come ye to the waters!" (55:1) We could quote almost endless examples.

What a blessing water is! No other liquid quenches thirst as does a drink of cool, clear, sparkling water. Cleanliness is said to be next to godliness, and it is water that keeps things clean. All vegetation would die if water dried up; man would perish and disappear from the earth without it. The soil would become powder dry and blow away if no rains fell. Nevertheless, we take it for granted; and seldom think of thanking God for water until a severe drought brings a water shortage, or by some chance, we find ourselves marooned in a desert where there is no water. When rains finally come, and we find our way to wells of water, we may remember then at least for a time to give thanks to God for the life-giving streams.

Water and fire are alike, in that both are not only beneficent, but also destructive. We remember that it was a flood which destroyed all mankind, except Noah and his family. The human race had become so evil that God repented having created man. We also remember that he promised never again to send a flood to destroy the world, and set his bow in the clouds as a reminder of the covenant. He has kept his promise, but there have been many destructive floods, often with great loss of life and property, in different areas of the world. We cannot understand such cataclysms of nature, but they bring to our minds the realization that man is but a puny creature in the presence of the awful power of God.

Sometimes extreme measures are required to make us recognize God's power. Bruce Barton, as a boy in Sunday school, did not like the pictures of Christ. He thought them weak and effeminate; the God he would worship was a real man, strong and virile. All of us desire a God of power, for no other kind of God could keep the worlds in their places. Our God must have such power that winds and waves obey him. He must be able to roll up a river to allow his people to pass through on dry ground; he must, in the midst of a storm at sea, say to the waves, "Be still!" and have the storm subside, and suddenly be followed by a great calm. He must send a great river thundering to the sea, but he must also provide "a spring of water whose waters fail not."

Gardens are beauty spots of the earth, and are the sources of life-giving foods. The author of Genesis wrote, "And a river went out of Eden to water the garden" (2:10), and the psalmist exulted: "Thou visitest the earth, and waterest it; thou greatly enrichest it with the river of God which is full of water" (65:9). Isaiah said, "Thou shalt be like a watered garden, and like a spring of water, whose waters fail not" (58:11). Just as the gardens of the world, watered by rivers, bear fruit to feed the bodies of men, so must our lives, watered by the streams of God's teaching, bear fruit for souls starved for the knowledge of God and his way of life.

Christ came that men should have life abundant, and joy is one element of the richness of Christian living. A follower of Christ should be the happiest of all people. "Thou shalt make them drink of the river of thy pleasures." Carl Sandburg wrote a prayer of thanks for "the gladness here where the sun is shining at evening on the weeds of the river." In the thirty-fifth chapter of Isaiah the prophet shows the joyful flourishing of God's kingdom, and rises to a climax in these words: "For in the wilderness shall waters break out, and streams in the desert. And the parched ground shall become a pool, and the thirsty land springs of water" (vs. 6). To a people knowing almost constantly the lack of water, a constant and plentiful supply constituted one of their greatest blessings.

Rivers are great thoroughfares of the world. Thousands of people have heard the messages of missionaries who made their way down rivers flowing into inaccessible places of continents to which there was no other approach. Rivers are thus highways of service to mankind. Sidney Lanier in his poem, "The Song of the Chattahoochee," pictures the river as it makes its way to the sea:

> But oh, not the hills of Habersham,
> And oh, not the valleys of Hall
> Await! I am fain for to water the plain.
> Downward the voices of Duty call—
> Downward, to toil and be mixed with the main,
> The dry fields burn, and the mills are to turn,
> And a myriad flowers mortally yearn,
> And the lordly main from beyond the plain
> Calls o'er the hills of Habersham,
> Calls through the valleys of Hall.

Just so our lives of service should flow through the world, until they find their way at last, to the infinity of God himself. Then we find the completion of life. John said, "They shall thirst no more." You remember that Isaiah shouted in a voice like a trumpet, "Ho, every one that thirsteth, come ye to the waters!" "Every one" means all of us—not a single one need be left out of that eternal joy. We need only thirst for the water of life which flows abundantly from the throne of God, enough for all the peoples of the world, and freely offered to give us everlasting life.

Let us hear the prayer of Francis of Assisi in praise and gratitude for water: "Praised be my Lord for our sister water, who is very serviceable to us, and humble and precious and clean."

Chapter VII

TREES

❖◇

"Thus saith the Lord God; I will also take of the highest branch of the high cedar, and will set it; I will crop off from the top of his young twigs a tender one, and will plant it upon an high mountain and eminent: In the mountain of the height of Israel will I plant it; and it shall bring forth boughs, and bear fruit, and be a goodly cedar: and under it shall dwell all fowl of every wing; in the shadow of the branches thereof shall they dwell. And all the trees of the field shall know that I the Lord have brought down the high tree, have exalted the low tree, have dried up the green tree, and have made the dry tree to flourish: I the Lord have spoken and have done it."

—Ezek. 17:22-24

"Even so every good tree bringeth forth good fruit, but a corrupt tree bringeth forth evil fruit. A good tree cannot bring forth evil fruit, neither can a corrupt tree bring forth good fruit. Every tree that bringeth not forth good fruit is hewn down, and cast into the fire. Wherefore by their fruits ye shall know them."

—Matt. 7:17-20

O*nce* I lived for many months in a section of the United States where for miles around, there were only cacti and other low shrubs that grow in semidesert country. The scrubby mesquite tree and an occasional dwarfed and misshapen willow-oak were the nearest thing to real trees in the area. As I had lived most of my life in a section of North Carolina where flourish most of the varieties of trees to be found in the United States—from small slender dogwoods, ash, and sourwood to lofty pines, majestic oaks, walnut, hickory, and maple trees—I naturally longed for the sight of a tall tree.

To me trees are another evidence of God's love for humanity. His word is full of allusions to them, from the tree of life in the garden of Eden to "the tree of life which bore twelve manner of fruits, and yielded her fruit every month and leaves of the tree were for the healing of the nations" (22:2), as John pictured it in the New Jerusalem of Revelation.

The psalmist likens the righteous man to "a tree planted by the rivers of water, that bringeth forth his fruit in his season" (1:3). Olive trees not only furnished oil, an essential element of food and a valued commercial commodity, but also symbolized the fruitfulness of the human family. The great cedars of Lebanon, buffeted and strengthened by winds and storms, were used in building the great temple. Much of the biblical country was dry and arid, and trees growing beside springs in the desert formed welcome oases to weary travelers and traders.

William Cullen Bryant once wrote, "The groves were God's first temples." The import of these words never impressed me so profoundly as when I stood, awed into silence, among the great Sequoia trees of California. Looking at the great trunks of the trees, which rise a hundred feet toward the sky like mighty pillars of a vast cathedral, and branch out into leafy finials like the delicate tracery of marble fretwork in Gothic ceilings, I felt like saying: "What is man, that thou art mindful of him?" (8:4.) I have never felt more humble, and yet I have seldom felt my soul more in the spirit of worship. I seemed to be standing in a mighty temple in the very presence of God.

How strong trees are! How often we have seen a great tree swaying, bowed by raging winds, then rising proudly unharmed by the mighty gales. It is said that in the days of great sailing vessels, the builders sought the lone pines that stood apart on the lofty hills of Norway to use as masts and spars. Those pines lower down, protected by other trees, were too soft and frail to bear the stress of storms at sea. The shipbuilders chose only those that by withstanding the terrific force of the elements had been proven strong. There is a lesson of life in this story. Most individuals whose lives are constantly sheltered and protected from the hardships of life are too soft and weak to stand up against difficulties; only those who have learned to stand firm when whipped and lashed by the storms of life's experiences, have grown strong enough to remain unshaken when beset by other, even fiercer tempests.

Coleridge said that "friendship is a sheltering tree," and Wordsworth speaks of "a brotherhood of venerable trees." Both of these poets have caught the friendly atmosphere of trees. On a hot summer day many a weary traveler finds coolness and refreshment in the dim, shady depths of a grove of trees. Children play beneath them; lovers whisper tender vows of love in their shelter; aged men and women rest and dream of the past in the recesses of their serene shadows. Trees minister to all ages and kinds of people as do kind and gentle friends—and what would life be without the tender ties of friendship? Jesus once said to his disciples, "Henceforth I call you not servants; . . . but I have called you friends" (John 15:15); and again he said, "Greater love hath no man than this, that a man lay down his life for his friends" (15:13). Is there someone who is lonely and longing for a friendly word or act? To show him friendship is to follow the Master's teachings and example.

God has put the capacity for seeing and appreciating beauty into the soul of every one of us. Only by his own volition and willful drabness of vision does a man shut his eyes to the beauty around him, and close his soul to its healing power. Throughout the year, in every season, trees add immeasurable beauty to the world around us. The grace and symmetry of the etching of bare boughs against a wintry sky transcends the skill of any earthly architect; the tender gray-green tints on newly budding trees lift and inspire our hearts. The multicolored flowering trees of spring give us joy, and the coolness of dense green foliage in midsummer heat comforts us. In autumn our souls are thrilled to almost unutterable joy by the glorious brilliant colors of the autumn trees, that look as if God had splashed all the colors in his unlimited paintbox upon the canvas of the forest. As autumn brings this glory to our lives, can we fail to see God in such beauty? Will it not lift our hearts in praise and adoration to the One who created it?

A vast majority of all homes in the world are built of wood that once grew as noble trees in the forests. The most powerful influence in our lives is the home and the tenderest associations we have go back to our homes. In Robert Frost's "Death of the Hired Man," Mary War-

45

ren defines home as "Something you somehow haven't to deserve." Yes, we do not always deserve good, Christian homes; but, how wonderful that God is a merciful Father who does not invariably deal with us on the basis of our just deserts, but is "plenteous in mercy"! If trees performed no other service to humanity than their transformation into homes, that alone would justify God in looking on their creation and calling it good.

Throughout the Bible the main emphasis in the figurative use of trees is that they must bear fruit. Matthew says, "Either make the tree good, and the fruit good; or else make the tree corrupt, and his fruit corrupt: for the tree is known by his fruit." (12:33.) The psalmist speaks of the tree "that bringeth forth his fruit in his season." We remember what Christ said when he went up to Jerusalem and found only leaves when he sought figs from the tree: "Let no fruit grow on thee henceforward for ever. And presently the fig tree withered away" (Matt. 21:19). Again Christ spoke of himself as the vine, and said, "Every branch in me that beareth not fruit he taketh away" (John 15:2). A tree bearing no fruit, when that is the purpose of its creation, has no right to cumber the ground. Must we be discarded because we bear no fruit, and if we are bearing fruit, is it good or corrupt? Do we bear leaves and fruit for the healing of the nations? It is by our fruit that we shall be judged.

Chapter VIII

BIRDS

❖❖

> "Yea, the sparrow hath found an house, and the swallow a nest for herself, where she may lay her young, even thine altars, O Lord of hosts, my King, and my God."
>
> —*Ps. 84:3*

> "But they that wait upon the Lord shall renew their strength; they shall mount up with wings as eagles; they shall run, and not be weary; and they shall walk, and not faint."
>
> —*Isa. 40:31*

*B*irds bring many beautiful things into our lives. Our ears are charmed by their glad songs at morning; by their tender, sleepy notes at evening; and wistful, haunting melodies in the moonlight. Many of them delight our eyes with their brilliant plumage, gleaming like jewels, among the green branches of the trees.

Many songbirds are shy; they withdraw into thick hedges or groves, away from the sight of humans, to pour out their melodies. The clear notes of the thrush or cardinal are musical evidence of their presence in the woods. Milton described the shyness of the nightingale thus:

> Sweet bird, that shuns't the noise of folly,
> Most musical, most melancholy!

The American mockingbird, on the other hand, will perch on the loftiest tip of the tallest tree or on the ridge of a high roof to sing songs of unrestrained rapture, to the delight of any who will listen.

After a long, cold winter the whole world joyously welcomes spring, and poets often show this joy reflected in the gladness of the birds' songs. In England the cuckoo's note is one of the first indications that spring is near; hence, naturally, many poets praise the cuckoo's coming. One of the earliest outstanding English lyrics begins:

> Sumer is icumen in;
> Lhude sing, cuccu!

And in the Song of Songs we read, "the time of the singing of birds is come, and the voice of the turtle is heard in our land" (2:12). A bit of Southern folklore declares that spring has come when the first red-breasted robin appears. A friendly bird, he hops fearlessly across the lawn seeking early worms, and cocking a bright eye at any passer by who will stay a reasonable distance away and keep comparatively quiet.

There is something in the songs of birds that often brings a feeling of sadness into our hearts. Poets suggest that the nightingale's song is sad, though naturalists do not agree. Milton calls it "melancholy." The whole atmosphere of Keat's "Ode to a Nightingale" is gentle sadness. We find ourselves experiencing much the same poignant emotion that filled the heart of Ruth as she "stood in tears amid the alien corn," listening to the almost unbearable sweetness of the song. Is this not the same nostalgic sadness that enters our hearts with any beautiful sight or sound? Beauty is so fleeting. We thrill to a dazzling sunset, but almost before we fully sense its glory, it has faded. A great chorus or a mighty symphony brings a tightness into the throat; but its sweetness lingers only briefly in the air. A lovely baby in its crib is so short a time a baby; youth, with its beauty and freshness, passes so quickly. Our hearts are saddened because all of these beautiful things are gone so soon. Thus it is as we linger in the woodland listening to the evening song of mockingbird, or go into the fields in early morning and hear the lark singing sweeter and clearer as he nears heaven's gate.

At times we allow ourselves to become out of tune with God's beauty in the world. In his poem "A Minor Bird," Robert Frost, with his uncanny ability to size up most human attitudes, went to the heart of the matter:

> I have wished a bird would fly away,
> And not sing by my house all day;

> Have clapped my hands at him from the door
> When it seemed as if I could bear no more.
>
> The fault must partly have been in me.
> The bird was not to blame for his key.
>
> And of course there must be something wrong
> In wanting to silence any song.[1]

How well the truth is expressed here. The soul that is in tune with nature and God finds its heart and soul responding to all beauty of sight and sound that God has created.

Have you ever been awakened in the early morning hours by a chorus of exultant bird songs? Donald Culross Peattie says that the time to hear the music of birds is between four and six in the morning. Yet most of us have become so indolent that the only emotion aroused in our hearts by such incomparable music is anger at being awakened so early. Dull, deaf souls that we are!

There is a parable for us in the singing of birds. Only a few birds have such songs as the mockingbird, the skylark, the nightingale, or even the briefer, but no less beautiful, single notes of the thrush or the cardinal; yet even those birds whose songs are confined to one weak chirp do not refuse to add their small parts to the great symphony. William Ernest Henley wrote:

> The nightingale has a lyre of gold,
>   The lark's is a clarion call,
> And the blackbird plays but a boxwood flute,
>   But I love him best of all.[2]

Though our contributions are no greater music than the chirp of the sparrow or the call of the lone sea bird, the great orchestra would be incomplete without these notes, and we would lose the joy and the satisfaction that comes from contributing our share in the symphony. This is again the parable of the unused talent.

In the Bible God teaches us many lessons from the birds. There are

[1] "A Minor Bird," from *Complete Poems of Robert Frost.* Copyright 1930, 1949 by Henry Holt and Company, Inc. Copyright 1936, 1948 by Robert Frost. By permission of the publishers.
[2] "To a Blackbird."

many times when we acknowledge God as the Creator of all the universes, the heavens, the earth, and all that is therein; yet we allow doubts to assail our mind as to his fatherhood, his love and care for us as individuals. We are so infinitesimal in the great scheme of creation that it is sometimes hard to believe that God takes account of each of us, and will hear and answer our petitions. There is great comfort in his words: "Are not two sparrows sold for a farthing? and one of them shall not fall on the ground without your Father" (Matt. 10:29).

Using a parable about birds, the psalmist taught the Hebrew people of long ago what a sanctuary the House of God might be in their lives. "Yea, the sparrow hath found an house, and the swallow a nest for herself, where she may lay her young, even thine altars, O Lord of hosts, my King, and my God." (Ps. 84:3). Today, when mankind needs more than ever a sanctuary where he may find peace, safety, and security, these words should fall with powerful force. Unless man makes the House of God his sanctuary, the life and teachings of Christ his pattern for living, there is no hope for salvation or even continued existence. If modern fathers and mothers would make God's Church the nest in which they would nurture their young, there would be an end to the problems of juvenile delinquency. Unless men and women are reborn into God's Church, and mankind makes God the fountain and source of all life, there is no hope for us.

The eagle is the king of birds, the only bird, so it is said, that can look unblinded into the very eye of the sun. He soars to vast heights, and builds his nest on the loftiest mountain peaks. Poets in the Bible and elsewhere have written of the power of the eagle and of its ability to reach great altitudes. These qualities should have deep meaning for us. All of us need to lift our eyes and to dream vaster dreams. No one can rise higher than his ideal; and an ideal must constantly beckon us on to greater heights. So Christ is the one perfect ideal, for no one can ever attain the perfection of Christ. The "Gleam" is constantly before us, leading us higher and higher to greater Christian living. It was something like this that inspired Isaiah to write: "But they that wait upon the Lord shall renew their strength; they shall mount up with wings as eagles; they shall run, and not be weary; and they shall walk, and not faint" (40:13).

It was the sight of a single sea bird winging its lonely way into a sunset sky that gave William Cullen Bryant great strength and courage at a time of doubt and indecision in his life. Most of us at some time or other have been faced with the question of making a change in our work or location which would probably affect our entire future lives. The thought which helped Bryant make his decision can guide us just as well.

> He, who, from zone to zone,
> Guides through the boundless sky thy certain flight,
> In the long way that I must tread alone,
> Will lead my steps aright.[3]

Yes, a loving Father gave great joy to his children when he put birds into the world. We can enjoy the beauty of the flashing jewel that is a hummingbird, darting from flower to flower in the garden; we can thrill to the sweetness of the mockingbird's song in the moonlight; we can regain our faith by watching a lone seafowl winging its solitary flight at sunset. God, who loves us, gave them all to us for our pleasure, that through them our thoughts would turn to him.

[3] "To a Waterfowl," stanza 8.

Chapter IX

GARDENS

❖❖❖

"And the Lord God planted a garden
eastward in Eden; and there he put the
man whom he had formed."

—Gen. 2:8

"For the Lord shall comfort Zion:
he will comfort all her waste places;
and he will make her wilderness like
Eden, and her desert like the garden of
the Lord; joy and gladness shall be found
therein, thanksgiving, and the voice of
melody."

—Isa. 51:3

T he crowning work of God, before he rested on the sabbath day, was
the creation of a perfect pair of humans. Since they were perfect, he
wished to place them in a suitable home. So eastward in Eden he planted
a garden, the perfect abode for humans made in the very image of God.

In his picture of the garden of Eden the author of Genesis shows us
little of the garden, except the trees. In *Paradise Lost,* however, Milton,
with all an Englishman's love for gardens, and with some of the most
vivid pictures of the lofty imagination of his poetic soul, gave us de-
tails of the beauty and abundance of the garden created to satisfy completely every physical need of man, as well as to delight all his finer
senses. The many flowers that Milton knew and loved in the English
gardens and countryside "Broidered the ground": many-hued iris, roses,
jasmine, violets, crocus, and hyacinth. There abounded sweet-smelling
herbs with which Eve decked her nuptial bed; nightingales lulled the
lovely pair to sleep with matchless wedding hymns. Food was there, to
be had for the taking.

There grew many trees giving welcome shade; and many, bearing
fruits for the delight of man's appetite. But also growing in the midst of

the garden were a tree of life and a tree of the knowledge of good and evil. This latter tree was the object of the only interdiction placed on man: "For in the day that thou eatest thereof thou shalt surely die" (Gen. 2:17). Let us never dismiss lightly the power of Satan; for he always attacks us in a vulnerable spot. He knew that he could tempt Eve with a promise of greater knowledge. It was also his Satanic shrewdness that made him select the subtle serpent, wisest animal in the garden, to tempt Eve beyond her power to resist. Afterward Eve led Adam to his fall by injecting into his heart a desire to know more than God's plan for man's knowledge. So it was in a garden that man's life began; in a garden his fall was accomplished; and there redemption began through repentance. Man had to leave the garden of Eden, and lose his idyllic state of pristine goodness in order to attain salvation through a more positive act of holiness—through freedom of will to choose either good or evil.

I think that there is in the souls of most people a desire to create something. Some write books, paint pictures, or compose great music. Others reproduce, performing the most Godlike act of creation—that of creating another human being. Many find great satisfaction in cultivating a garden. Bronson Alcott, who learned much of his philosophy from growing things, once said:

> Who loves a garden still his Eden keeps,
> Perennial pleasures plants, and wholesome harvests reaps.

There is little more thrilling than planting a seed, and then watching the miracle of growth that follows—from the first thrust of tiny sprouts through the brown soil, as the green hint becomes a pair of leaves. What a marvel it is that from a tiny brown seed no larger than a grain of sand can come roots, strong stems, green leaves, and flowers of every imaginable hue. How can anyone walk through a garden when flowers are in bloom, or vegetables are ripening and not believe in a powerful and loving God who gives so much beauty and goodness to his children?

All of God's creations are orderly and systematic. The orderliness that produces only an iris from an iris bulb, and pansies from pansy seeds, never mixing or confusing them, can come only from the mind of the same Creator who fixed the stars in their orbits, and the suns and planets in their paths, so that among the countless billions that light the sky, none go astray to disturb the system of all the ages. God created them all—from a seed no larger than a mustard seed to the brightest sun in the heavens; and as we contemplate the wonder of them all, we worship and adore the Father who made them.

Plants cannot grow in our gardens without work. When God drove Adam and Eve from the garden of Eden and decreed that man should earn his bread by the sweat of his brow, he was pronouncing no curse on work. Work is essential to life; throughout the Bible the gospel of work is taught, and idleness is identified with evil. Work is a great panacea for loneliness, heartbreak, or for general dissatisfaction with life. Many a lonely soul has forgotten his loneliness by spending hours digging and planting in a garden, and then has found his way back to God and a happy life by sharing with his friends, and other lonely or needy ones, the flowers and vegetables he has grown.

To grow the right products it is necessary to know and select the best seeds. Russell Conwell, a great preacher of other years, once said:

> I ask not for a larger garden,
> But for finer seeds.[1]

In these lines lies a great lesson of life. How many of us often sigh for larger fields, deceiving ourselves into a disillusionment that if we had a larger garden in which to work, the results of our efforts would be greater. If we could only understand with Conwell that it is the kind of seeds we sow that determines the harvest. The majority of us will not sow in wide fields, and most of us will have only a small garden. If each of us plants in his small space only the finest seeds of love, truth, goodness, and beauty, the harvest from that small area will spread out in far-reaching and ever-widening fields, until the whole world is blest and saved by the products from the many small gardens of the world.

We should work and watch that no seeds except those of righteousness take root in the gardens of our souls, so that they may produce only good grain—fruit that will ripen in the hearts and lives of those around us, and therefore in the everlasting kingdom of God.

> First the blade, and then the ear,
> Then the full corn shall appear:
> Lord of harvest, grant that we
> Wholesome grain and pure may be.

[1] "My Prayer." Used by permission.

Chapter X

FLOWERS

❖❖

> "Consider the lilies how they grow:
> they toil not, they spin not; and yet I
> say unto you, that Solomon in all his
> glory was not arrayed like one of these."
>
> *—Luke 12:27*

> "I am the rose of Sharon, and the lily
> of the valleys."
>
> *—Song of Songs 2:1*

The slogan of florists, "Say it with flowers," has become so familiar that we miss its full connotation. The words meet our eyes from advertisements in magazines and newspapers; they are printed on florists' windows and delivery trucks; billboards blazon them along highways. Yet we are hardly conscious of seeing them. However, if we would really stop to think about their meaning, we would find them rich in the power of suggestion. How many things a flower can say! A single blossom in the sickroom of a friend carries a message of cheer and love altogether out of proportion to the size and value of the gift. Flowers have special meanings for many occasions—from a lover to his sweetheart, from a husband to his wife, from a pupil to his teacher; a flower placed on the altar in the sanctuary on Sunday morning or one sent to comfort a stricken heart saddened by the loss of a beloved one. What a poor world it would be, if we did not have flowers to say to others things that often cannot be said so well in any other way.

Elsewhere we have spoken of the peace and joy that can be attained by the cultivation of flowers. One of the loveliest pictures in *Paradise Lost* is that of Eve—beautiful, pure, and innocent, before sin entered her soul—as she works among her flowers, tying up her roses, and— somewhat symbolically—supporting the fragile stems of other flowers. Someone has said that we are closer to God in a garden then anywhere else. Certainly many a man or woman has found comfort in sorrow, and physical and spiritual restoration by hours spent among flowers.

What would spring be if the trees, fields, and gardens did not blossom forth in all the marvelous colors and patterns of thousands of flowers. One of my loveliest memories is of a spring evening in the country near San Antonio, Texas, when I stood looking across a field carpeted with bluebonnets, Indian paintbrush, little wild sunflowers, and many other native wildflowers to where an old Spanish mission stood silhouetted against an evening sky. To add a final note of breath-taking beauty was the silver thread of a new moon just above the old tower. Such loveliness fills our hearts with thankfulness to our Father who created it. God could have made a world which would have supplied all the things essential for keeping us alive, and left out beauty. But he did not. Let us thank him with all our hearts for one of his extras—beautiful flowers.

Thomas Gray spoke of flowers "born to blush unseen," and Wordsworth in his "Intimations on Immortality" said:

> To me the meanest flower that blows can give
> Thoughts that do often lie too deep for tears.

A host of golden daffodils "dancing and fluttering in the breeze" can set our hearts dancing with them. James Russell Lowell in his poem "To a Dandelion," wrote of that flower we call a weed and work zealously to uproot from our lawns:

> Dear common flower, that grow'st beside the way,
> Fringing the dusty road with harmless gold.

He said of that "gold":

> Though most hearts never understand
> To take it at God's value, but pass by
> The offered wealth with unrewarded eye.

The world would lose much of its glory if the lowly flowers ceased to bloom. If the dandelion or the wild violet should refuse to bloom because it was not a gorgeous rose or an exotic orchid, the loss would be immeasurable. These small flowers seem to me to be like the one-talent servant. And are not most of us one-talent people? If we hide our talents in a napkin, refusing to use them because they are not ten talents, our share in the growth of God's kingdom will be forever lost. His kingdom will come, but only those who use their talents, though they may seem to be no more important than the tiniest flower, will have a part in bringing it to pass.

Have you ever thought of the contribution that fragrance makes to our pleasure? Walter Pater wrote: "Nothing is more fit for that delight than to know what flowers and plants do best perfume the air." And someone else said, "There can be no perfect flower without perfume." Shakespeare's sonnet says:

> The rose looks fair, but fairer we it deem,
> For that sweet odour which doth in it live.

The influence of a lovely Christian life is like the perfume of a flower. Its beauty enters subtly and almost insensibly into our consciousness, and we find ourselves yearning to be like such a person, or quietly seeking to emulate the goodness that emanates like a delicate perfume from his life. Someone has called this fragrance the aura of influence of a holy life as the "flowers that do perfume the air."

In an age such as this when people are restless, worried, fearful, and tormented with anxiety and insecurity, what better prescription is there for freedom from these cares than Christ's words to his disciples? "Consider the lilies how they grow: they toil not, they spin not, and yet I say unto you that Solomon in all his glory was not arrayed like one of these."

Today is not a time for smugness or complacency. The only way we can rid our souls of burdens of fear and anxiety and our minds from stress and nervous tension is to trust implicitly in him. We must believe with all our hearts that he, without whose care not even the tiniest flower blooms, watches over and cares for all his children—even the most unimportant.

There are some people who still say they do not believe in miracles, or that the days of miracles are past, in spite of the many miracles of science, healing, and modern inventions that take place every single day. But what miracle achieved by man can equal the miracle of a growing flower? How roots, stems, green leaves, and brilliant colored blossoms can develop from a tiny seed, so small that the naked eye cannot distinguish it from the soil around it, is "miracle enough to stagger sextillions of infidels." Listen to Tennyson as he looks upon a tiny flower springing from a crevice in a stone wall:

> Flower in the crannied wall,
> I pluck you out of the crannies;
> I hold you here, root and all, in my hand,
> Little flower—but if I could understand
> What you are, root and all, and all in all,
> I should know what God and man is.

However, it seems to me that no one has attained a more reverent appreciation and greater mystic revelation of the lowly plants in the whole scheme of God's creation than did Walt Whitman when he wrote these lines in his "Song of Myself":

I believe a leaf of grass is no less than the journey-work of the stars.

. . . .

And the running blackberry would adorn the parlors of heaven.

Silence Medicine

By GEORGE M. ADAMS

NOISE AND NERVES never to be very good friends. probably because they have ver seemed to understand ch other. More likely because they are fundamentally very opposite in nature.

Noise is never so content as when troubling nerves. Nerves are never so happy as when are a hundred miles or so y from noise.

. M. Adams

about two-thirds of the nquilizing" pill factories ld go out of business, this d would be a happier place people to live in. There is nuch noise about. The poor es get tired and shaky. e the call for pills.

ny times the greatest cine in the world for "oute-way" nerves is Silence cine.

Where you and noise are not together. Where you can say to your nerves: "Well, nerves, here we are—out with the trees, and ground, and animals, and birds, and—Silence."

How wonderful is silence! How the odds and ends are gathered up—in Silent Land. How affairs get quckly straightened out—where noise is absent.

The cheapest and most valuable medicine in the world is the silence medicine.

Why not prescribe it for yourself? Anyway, for a weekend!

The Four-C

By H. I. PHILLIPS

("ASKED HOW the public could get TV evils corrected, Dr. Stanton, head of CBS, replied, 'It's as simple as a four-cent stamp and a letter.' ")

DEAR DR. STANTON: Okay, here is my four-cents worth:—

1—Don't you think that in the Perry Mason show the district attorney should be allowed to win ONCE in a

THIS TEST PROVES HOW LIFE FILTERS BEST OF ALL!

1. The filter on the right is Life's new Millecel Super Filter. On the left, we test the best of the other filters.

2. Equal amounts of test solution are dropped onto each filter. Now see how Life gives least tar, least nicotine!

3. After only a few drops, the other filter fails. Lets drops pass right through!

4. But Life's exclusive new Millecel Super Filter absorbs drop after drop after drop.

Proof positive Life is best! Life gives least tar, least nicotine of all cigarettes! Change to new Life!

Today America's smokers are chang
new Life! Because Life has the Mil
proved to give you the least tar, lea
cigarette—least tar, least nicotine of

Chapter XI

SUNSHINE AND CLOUDS

❖❖❖

> "Truly the light is sweet, and a pleasant thing it is for the eyes to behold the sun."
>
> —*Eccl. 11:7*

> "Praised be my Lord God, with all His creatures, and especially our brother the Sun, who brings us the day and who brings us the light: fair is he, and he shines with a very great splendor."
>
> —*Francis of Assisi*

> "If all the skies were sunshine,
> Our faces would be fain
> To feel once more upon them
> The cooling plash of rain." [1]
>
> —*Henry van Dyke*

O*n* the first day of the Creation God said, "Let there be light," and he placed the great light in the heavens to give illumination by day, and the lesser lights to give light by night. From that time, throughout all ages, the greater light, the sun, has been the source of all light and heat; and all living things have owed to it their growth and development. Hence it is not strange that primitive and pagan peoples, not knowing God, the Creator of the sun, turned their adoration and worship to the sun itself. Centuries before Christ an unknown Egyptian writer, in his poem, "A Hymn to Amen-Ra, the Sun God," addressed him as:

> Lord of truth, father of the gods,
> Maker of men, fashioner of animals,

[1] "If All the Skies," used by permission of the publishers, Charles Scribner's Sons.

Lord of corn,

．　　　．　　　．　　　．　　　．　　　．　　　．　　　．

Maker of things below and of things above.

This pagan poet, worshiping the most powerful force he knew, attributed to the sun-god many attributes of our Father, the Christian God—power, sweetness, radiance, and beauty—but here, as everywhere in pagan literature, we find everything ending in despair, pessimism, and futility. These people did not know God, the Creator of heaven and earth, and the loving Father of mankind. P. E. Lindley, for many years beloved dean of High Point College, used to say to his students: "There is something in the soul of every man that leads him to worship something. The Christian soul recognizes in God the one Divine Being worthy of his worship, the highest that he can think, and owns Him as his Savior."

Like so many other blessings that God gives to us, we take sunshine for granted, seldom stopping to say, "Thank you, God," when we awaken to see the glorious rays of light flooding our rooms. Physicians say we would feel much better physically if after awakening, we would lie quietly for a few minutes before arising. Religious psychiatrists urge us to start our days by spending those few minutes in prayer and the repetition of verses of scripture. I truly believe that our entire day would go better if, before getting out of bed, we would include among our verses the words from Ecclesiastes, "Truly the light is sweet, and a pleasant thing it is for the eyes to behold the sun" (11:7).

Milton shows us a beautiful picture in *Paradise Lost,* of Adam and Eve as they step forth, hand in hand, from their bower in the glorious morning light. In thoughts which Milton borrowed from the nineteenth Psalm, Adam joined his voice in unison with all his creatures in exaltation and praise of his Creator. He began:

> Thou Sun, of this great World both eye and soul,
> Acknowledge him thy Greater; sound his praise
> In thy eternal course, both when thou climb'st,
> And when high noon hast gained, and when thou fall'st.

As we thank God at every meal for the food which we are about to eat, we should remember that there is no food which does not require sunshine for its production. Maltbie D. Babcock wrote:

And back of the mill is the wheat and the shower
And the sun and the Father's will.

In the springtime the whole world flames with every imaginable color. Plum, pear, and peach trees are clouds of white and pink; flowering trees are drifts of color from palest pink to flaming red. Fields and gardens are like an oriental carpet—the gold of daffodils, myriads of multicolored pansies, tulips of all colors like inverted bells, and everywhere masses of forsythia like spots of sunshine.

Sunshine and happiness are synonymous. A happy person radiates happiness as the sun radiates light and warmth, and attracts others even as sunshine calls us out to bask in its rays. Each of us knows someone who draws us to him because of the radiance of his character. People in my town will not soon forget the minister who shed throughout the whole town the radiance of his consecrated, sunny, Christian personality. He made happy people happier, troubled people less troubled, and sad people hopeful; because of him many bad people turned to a better way of life. J. M. Barrie could have had him in mind when he wrote: "Those who bring sunshine to the lives of others cannot keep it from themselves." There is a homely proverb, "Honey catches more flies than vinegar." Let us paraphrase it by saying that a radiant, happy Christian will spread the love of God wherever he goes; while a sour, solemn, gloomy individual will drive everybody from him and the brand of Christianity he practices.

When Christ was in the world, he was a sunny, happy person. He drew all people to him. He was a welcome guest everywhere: at a wedding feast, at banquets, in homes where there was illness or death, and even in the homes of publicans and sinners. His friends invited him repeatedly into their homes. The fact that children loved him and climbed on his knees was one of the greatest tests of his lovable character; for children love only those who are sunny and lovable.

Life, however, is not made up entirely of sunshiny days; in the world of nature, too, there must be rainy ones. Once I spent several months in the Southwest during a very dry period. In all the time that I was there, there was only one heavy shower and one misty morning when the air was dampened for a few hours. How I yearned for a cloudy day. I became tired of cloudless blue skies day after day. Vegetation dried up except where there was irrigation, and severe dust storms were frequent. Yes, much as we love the sunshine, we also love the clouds. Henry van Dyke's words are true:

> If all the skies were sunshine,
>   Our faces would be fain
> To feel once more upon them
>   The cooling plash of rain.

There is great beauty in a cloudy sky. The gorgeous colors of a sunset are painted on clouds; the beauty of a moonlit sky is greater when the moon rides in and out of light, broken clouds. There is majesty in storm clouds riven by jagged streaks of lightning; there is delicacy in fleecy flakes of clouds drifting across a blue sky.

How wonderful it is that God has surrounded us with so much beauty! Let us thank him continually that he is beauty-loving and that he planted in our souls the capacity to see and enjoy beauty.

> For the beauty of the earth,
>   For the glory of the skies,
> For the love which from our birth
>   Over and around us lies:
> Lord of all, to Thee we raise
> This our hymn of grateful praise.
>
> For the beauty of each hour
>   Of the day and of the night,
> Hill and vale, and tree and flower,
>   Sun and moon, and stars of light,
> Lord of all, to Thee we raise
> This our hymn of grateful praise.

Don Knight

Chapter XII

RAIN AND SNOW

"For as the rain cometh down, and the snow from heaven, and returneth not thither, but watereth the earth, and maketh it bring forth and bud, that it may give seed to the sower, and bread to the eater."

—*Isa. 55:10*

"I will give you the rain of your land in his due season, the first rain and the latter rain, that thou mayest gather in thy corn, and thy wine, and thine oil."

—*Deut. 11:14*

"He giveth snow like wool."

—*Ps. 147:16*

E*verything* in the world is affected by the weather. All life would soon cease without rain. Only a season or two of no rain would be sufficient for all vegetation to die, and the time would be short until animal life would also cease to exist. On the other hand, man could be destroyed by floods and cloudbursts except that God promised Noah that never again would he destroy all people by water. God said to Noah, "I do set my bow in the cloud, and it shall be for a token of a covenant between me and the earth. . . . The waters shall no more become a flood to destroy all flesh" (Gen. 9:13, 15).

Since much of the land where the Israelites dwelt was desert, water was a precious commodity. Hence, rain is frequently mentioned in the Bible. The Israelites were primarily a rural people who depended on

71

the land for food for themselves and their sheep and cattle. They fed upon the fruits of vine and tree; wine furnished their drink and was a great source of their revenue. There were frequent droughts followed by famines. In the light of these conditions, God's goodness and mercy in his promises of rain become more meaningful. Time and again he promised to the people the rain so essential for preservation of their lives and crops. In return for obedience to his commandments, God promised to Moses on Sinai, "Then I will give you rain in due season, and the land shall yield her increase, and the trees of the field shall yield their fruit" (Lev. 26:4).

One of the vivid stories of the Old Testament is that concerning a great rain. We remember the prolonged drought in Israel during the reign of the evil Ahab when Elijah was the prophet of God. It was after this drought had lasted for years that there occurred the great contest over the true God between the prophets of Baal and Elijah. It went on all day, ending when fire came from heaven and consumed Elijah's sacrifice, and the people took up the shout, "The Lord he is the God!" Then Elijah went up into Mount Carmel to pray. Seven times he sent his servant to scan the heavens, and the seventh time he brought to Elijah the news of a cloud no bigger than a man's hand. Elijah sent word to Ahab to hasten home while there was still time. In the meantime the heavens became black with clouds and wind, "and there was a great rain."

David's memory of his life as a shepherd lad on a hillside made him understand what showers meant to the thirsty land. In his later life when he wrote many of the psalms, he lifted his voice in sincere thankfulness to God for refreshing showers: "Thou waterest the ridges thereof abundantly: thou settlest the furrows thereof; thou makest it soft with showers" (Ps. 65:10). Again it must have been the glad heart of David the shepherd, concerned about the food for his flocks, that caused him to sing of God's goodness poured out upon the earth: "He shall come down like rain upon the mown grass: as showers that water the earth" (Ps. 72:6).

God in his great goodness has sent the "rain in due season" through all time and in all lands. Though there may be droughts or famines, floods or other catastrophes in some areas, God has never failed his promises to show mercy. The rains will fall on the just and the unjust; the land will produce again, or another land will provide a refuge; the floods will recede, and life will continue. And so the cycles succeed one another. How can one fail to recognize and acknowledge God as the Maker and Preserver of all things? He has always kept the processes of nature in ceaseless and rhymthic operation.

Rain is beautiful. Showers veil the world in a silvery mist; a rainbow spans the heavens with an arch containing all the beautiful tints of the spectrum. When we awake in the morning following a shower during the night and see a refreshed, sparkling world cleansed of all the dust and grime of past days, the words of William L. Stidger come to our minds:

> I saw God wash the world last night
> With his sweet showers on high,
> And then, when morning came, I saw
> Him hang it out to dry.[1]

Can you think of a more suitable metaphor than "showers of blessings"?

Of all nature's phenomena, the most thrilling is snow. Children shout with glee as the first flakes fall, and there is enough of the child in the hearts of most adults to cause them to share the pleasure of the children as commonplace landscapes are transformed into veritable fairylands by the "frolic architecture of the snow."

Poets have written some of their loveliest lines in lyric description of the beauty of snow. Perhaps the best-known snow poem is "Snow-Bound," Whittier's story in verse of the life of a New England family while they were snow-bound by a fall of snow such as winter occasionally brings to that part of the country. In well-chosen words Whittier describes the beginning of the storm:

> Unwarmed by any sunset light
> The gray day darkened into night,
> A night made hoary with the swarm
> And whirl dance of the blinding storm,
> As zigzag, wavering to and fro,
> Crossed and re-crossed the winged snow:
> And ere the early bedtime came
> The white drift piled the windowframe,
> And through the glass the clothes-line posts
> Looked in like tall and sheeted ghosts.

[1] "I Saw God Wash the World Last Night." Used by permission of Mrs. William L. Stidger.

Elinor Wylie has made the whiteness of snow whiter, and its softness softer in her poem "Velvet Shoes." Nobody has caught the silence of a snowy evening as Robert Frost did in "Stopping by Woods on a Snowy Evening." In the Bible are numerous allusions to snow. The psalmist said, "He giveth snow like wool" (147:16).

New-fallen snow is the perfect symbol for complete purity. Shakespeare said, "As chaste as unsunn'd snow," and Isaiah, in an unparalleled picture of God's forgiveness, said, "Though your sins be as scarlet, they shall be as white as snow" (1:18). David, in the agony of his soul, as he prays for God's forgiveness for his terrible sin, cried, "Wash me, and I shall be whiter than snow!" (Ps. 51:7.)

Rain and snow—natural blessings from the storehouse of the loving Father, from whom comes "every good and perfect gift." Job praised him for these blessings when he said, "For he saith to the snow, Be thou on the earth; likewise to the small rain, and to the great rain of his strength!" (37:6.)

Chapter XIII

PRING

❖❖❖❖❖❖❖❖❖❖❖❖❖❖❖❖❖❖❖❖❖❖❖❖❖❖❖❖❖❖❖❖

"Spring had come
Like the silver needle-note of a fife,
Like a white plume and a green lance
    and a glittering knife
And a jubilant drum." [1]

—Joseph Auslander

"For, lo, the winter is past, the rain is over and gone; The flowers appear on the earth; the time of the singing of birds is come, and the voice of the turtle is heard in our land; The fig tree putteth forth her green figs, and the vines with the tender grape give a good smell."

—Song of Songs 2:11-13

If winter comes, can spring be far behind?" the poet asked in an exultant climax to one of the world's great nature lyrics.

How we welcome spring! I do not believe that I should like to live long in a land where one season goes into another with little change of temperature or vegetation. I remember once that I did live for a time in a place where brilliant colored flowers bloomed most of the winter. I realized then the full meaning of Browning's

Oh, to be in England,
Now that April's there.

And I yearned to see our elm tree bursting into leaf, to see a blossoming pear tree, and a modest buttercup instead of the gaudy blooms about me.

[1] "Steel," used by permission.

Winters in the British Isles are likely to be long, cold, and grim. Rain, ice, and snow make going abroad a venturesome feat for even the hardiest; the days are short and gloomy; daylight comes late in the morning, and darkness has fallen by the middle of the afternoon. So it is not strange that people begin to yearn for long, sunny, warm days, singing birds, and blossoming flowers; and that from earliest times poets have sung longingly of the coming of spring. While the reputation of the cuckoo is not above reproach, the world welcomes his cheery call as one of the first harbingers of spring.

> Hark! how the jolly cuckoos sing,
> "Cuckoo," to welcome in the spring!

happily sang John Lyly centuries ago.

Winter has its beauties and its joys; but after weeks of cold, icy weather, and dark, gloomy days, how happy we are to throw open our doors and windows to the glorious sunlight and let the balminess of the spring breezes blow all the cold and dreariness away. The songbirds come back, and the loveliness of the gentle spring flowers thrill our hearts. We breathe deeply to catch the delicate fragrance of woods flowers—the trillium, violets, and the arbutus. We see the sunshine in the daffodils as they "dance and flutter in the breeze"; tulips are like "bubbles of blown-glass"; crocuses, pansies, iris, and myriads of other spring flowers make a mosaic pattern that no artists can ever reproduce. Our hearts are lifted in gratitude to the Giver of every good and perfect gift. We worship the Creator with our love for his creations. Cannot every one who has felt in his soul the bleakness of the winter of despair, grief, or lack of faith find his joy restored and his faith revived by the beauty around him—evidence of God's bountiful love? How simply Katherine Tynan Hinkson said it:

> All in the April evening,
>   April airs were abroad,
> I saw the sheep with their lambs,
>   And thought on the Lamb of God.[2]

The pagans celebrated the coming of spring by setting aside a day of feasting and joy in honor of Eos, the goddess of spring. They called

[2] "Sheep and Lambs," used by permission of the publishers, Macmillan & Company, Ltd.

the day Eostre. When the Son of God triumphed over the grave, laying aside the earthly body, and coming forth in all the radiance and glory of the risen Christ, how fitting it was that his followers should transform this pagan celebration into the most solemn holiday of all the Christian calendar. Christmas is a blessed, sacred time, but its meaning would be lost without Easter, when that same Jesus revealed himself as Master of life and death and gave us the wonderful truth of immortality.

Spring is a time of beginning anew as are a new year and a new day. All nature puts on new apparel. We also are tired of winter garments, and at the first hint of balmy weather, blossom forth in spring outfits. The housewife turns her house upside down in a spring cleaning; the farmer rakes off and burns the dead weeds, fallen sticks, and boughs broken by winter storms, in order to cleanse the soil and make it ready for new crops. It would do us good to have a spring revival in our spiritual lives. We need occasionally to turn the rooms of the temple of our bodies upside down and clear out many wrong ideas, prejudices, and low aims; and replace them with spiritual concepts more in keeping with the teachings of the Master. Sometimes it would be helpful to burn away the dross of evil desires and low thoughts, and so cleanse our minds and souls that higher, nobler dreams and ambitions might flourish and make us more Christlike. A good spring cleaning might change our lives.

Springtime is seedtime. It is the testing time for the harvest that is to follow. Is the soil prepared for the sowing? We remember our Lord's parable and relate it to our own lives. Will some of the seeds be so choked and killed by weeds of worldliness and sinful living that it is impossible for them to take root? Will the soil seem to be so well-prepared that the growth of the new plants will appear miraculous, then all at once begin to wilt and die because the preparation was only on the surface; underneath remained the hard rocky base of insincerity, disbelief, or hypocrisy? Or will the seeds of goodness, truth, and godliness fall into a soil so mellowed by God's love and power that the whole community is sweetened and blessed by the beauty and fragrance of the fruit and the bounty of the harvest?

The assurance of the coming of spring is consolation on the darkest, coldest, and dreariest day of winter. It may at times be so slow in coming that we begin to wonder if it will ever arrive again. But it has never failed. We hold fast to God's promise to Noah: "While the earth remaineth, seedtime and harvest, and cold and heat, and summer and winter, and day and night shall not cease" (Gen. 8:22). Margaret E. Sangster said:

> Never yet was a springtime,
>
> . . . .
>
> When the buds forgot to blow.[3]

And Whittier, with the simple and childlike faith so characteristic of his life and writings, wrote:

> With the calm patience of the woods I wait
> For leaf and blossom when God gives us Spring!

So with thanks to God we thrill as spring comes marching over hill and dale, waving its banners of blooming trees and shrubs. As it arrives it spreads a carpet of flowers more regal than any carpet spread to welcome an earthly queen, and breathes a fragrance sweeter than the traditional perfumes of Araby; and we join our voices with the voice of the singer of old: "For, lo, the winter is past, the rain is over and gone; The flowers appear on the earth; the time of the singing of birds is come, and the voice of the turtle is heard in our land; the fig tree putteth forth her green figs, and the vines with the tender grape give a good smell."

---

[3] "Awakening," used by permission of the author.

Today's Talk—By George Matthew Adams
Rise Above It! 2-'54

One of the most inspiring of American poems is that one by Longfellow—"A Psalm of Life." It has given a spiritual lift to millions, and it has been memorized by countless numbers. I once read that it was written when the poet was recovering from a deep depression.

G. M. Adams

After writing it he set it aside, and refused to have it published, but when it was, it swept the country, was recited in schools and was translated into many languages. Many a great leader today can recall reading it, and memorizing it, in his youth.

All of us at times have experienced a depression of spirit. Longfellow's poem has helped us to Rise Above It and "learn to labor and to wait." We may know that "growing pains" are at work when we feel low and discouraged. With faith and courage we can be assured that better days are ahead.

It was while John Howard Payne was in a hotel in Paris, alone and homesick, that he was inspired to write one of the most beloved songs in the world—"Home, Sweet Home." Great crowds have been brought to tears during its singing by great artists. There's a line in the Bible that has always inspired me. It reads: "Weeping may endure for a night, but joy cometh in the morning."

The time of all times not to give up is when you are despondent and discouraged. Rise Above It! It was during such a time that W. E. Henley wrote his immortal "Invictus," in which he said that he was the Captain of his soul. He was in a hospital at the time and was threatened with the loss of his leg. But Henley triumphed—and so can we! No matter what the circumstance, we can Rise Above It and be, with Henley, the Master of our fate.

s of Oklahoma City, grand
f the lodge from 15 original

In the past exalted rulers' class,
hich was initiated this week, are
ohn Bauer Jr.; Robert Delama-
r, John E. Eckstine, Lincoln E.
.ouck, Jerome Kaplan, Robert G.
ipman, Edward S. Mewmyer,
red Orbach, Joseph I. Smink,
.obert P. Watson, Henry H.
oung, George H. Hebard and
ouis A. Michaels.

★

before federal and state admini-
strative commissions and agencies.

9. "Removal of the judicial
system from politics by adoption
of the Pennsylvania plan for the
selection of judges.

10. "Improvement of the courts
of the magistrates and justices of
the peace by consolidating districts
and reducing the number of such
officials, increasing their educa-
tional requirements, substituting
salaries for the present fee system,
and reducing costs in such courts."

—Evening News Photo

a City, grand exalted ruler
Robins, right, at a Past
ght are: Howard R. Davis
State Elks president, and

Chapter XIV

AUTUMN

❖❖❖

"We lack but open eye and ear
To find the Orient's marvel here;
The still small voice in autumn's hush,
Yon maple wood the burning bush."

—John Greenleaf Whittier

"Say not ye, There are yet four
months, and then cometh harvest? behold, I say unto you, Lift up your eyes,
and look on the fields; for they are white
already to harvest."

—John 4:35

*T*o some people autumn is a time of dying leaves and fading flowers; to others it is a time of fulfillment, of ripening, and gathering in the harvest fruits.

Heap high the farmer's wintry hoard!
Heap high the golden corn!
No richer gift has Autumn poured
From out her lavish horn!

Truly, each season has its own beauty: winter, the snowy landscape, the grace of bare trees etched against a gray sky; spring, myriad shades of green, budding trees and tender hues of spring blossoms; summer, laden fruit trees and the hot blaze of summer flowers. October, however, brings the exhilaration of frosty mornings and paints the woods with more colors than the most ingenious artist can mix on his palette. Edna St. Vincent Millay, in breathless rapture before woods that "ache and sag and all but cry out with color," expressed her ecstasy thus:

> Lord, I do fear
> Thou'st made the world too beautiful this year.[1]

The beauty of autumn is the beauty of maturity. Someone has said that a girl of sixteen is always beautiful because all youth is beautiful; but the beauty of a woman of sixty is the beauty of a lovely soul that illuminates her face and shines through her kindly eyes. Her beauty comes from a life of unselfishness, service to others, and of dedication to the holiest things of life. Its glory is the glory of accomplishment. So it is with autumn; the fruit has ripened, and nature has reached her climax.

"The pastures are clothed with flocks; the valleys also are covered over with corn; they shout for joy, they also sing." (Ps. 65:13.)

The abundance and fulfillment of harvest at autumn do not happen by accident; they come about because of careful preparation and constant attention. In Ecclesiastes we read, "In the morning sow thy seed, and in the evening withhold not thine hand" (11:6). Whittier wrote in his "For an Autumn Festival":

> Once more the liberal year laughs out
> O'er richer stores than gems or gold;
> Once more with harvest-song and shout
> Is Nature's bloodless triumph told.

In springtime all the seeds must be sown with care; and the growing plants carefully pruned, sprayed, weeded, and cultivated through long, hot summer days to bring the reward of laden fruit trees, full granaries, and a plentiful supply of food to feed one's own family and to contribute to the hungry and needy folk in the world.

There are many lovely symbolic ideas of autumn. Robert Southey wrote of the "harvest-time of love." Youth and springtime are the time of mating. One of the most beautiful things in the world is a fine young couple in love culminating in marriage. Most brides are beautiful, and their photographs appearing in newspapers are charming. But one of the loveliest pictures published is that of a couple who have lived together forty, fifty, and sometimes even more years. These marriages with their offspring, children of such long-lasting devotion, compose the most stabi-

---

[1] "God's World" from *Renascence*, Harper's, copyright 1913, 1941 by Edna St. Vincent Millay.

lizing influence in a world where matrimony is too often entered into lightly, and tossed aside with equal frivolity. No nation can last long when family life declines. When young couples build their marriages on God's laws and let him guide their lives, they may be sure of reaping a harvest of love as the autumn of life approaches.

In the recurring seasons we again note the certainty of the laws of nature—God's laws. Occasionally the summer heat seems to remain long into the autumn months, and the foliage seems to retain too long the green of summer. We may be led to think that there will be no crisp fall days, and that the leaves will not put on their customary fall attire—they will merely turn a lifeless brown, dry up, and fall. But suddenly one morning we awaken to find a frosty crispness in the air, the bright blue of an October sky. Almost without our being aware of the approaching change, we realize that about us trees are clothed in crimson, gold, brown, and every shade between; and we move in the golden glow of their reflection. Autumn is here in all its glory. As we read in Genesis, "While the earth remaineth, seedtime and harvest, and cold and heat, and summer and winter, and day and night shall not cease" (8:22). Once more our faith in the unfailing truth of God's word is firmly grounded. God rules his world with complete orderliness.

The most helpful symbol of autumn in our lives is that of reaping time. At harvest time the eternal truth of reaping what we have sowed is proved. Only good seed can produce good crops. Men do not "gather grapes of thorns or figs of thistles." If young people could only learn this lesson before they have sowed the wrong kind of seed, how great a difference it would make. Some do learn this lesson early and sow only good seed; but many come to reaping time to find that the tares and weeds of evil, which were planted along the way, have grown with the good seed, and have dwarfed and diminished the good harvest.

The complete results of no man's life can be known here; only the Son of God can say at the end, "It is finished!" But in the Bible are repeated allusions to the "plenteous harvest" and the need for laborers in the field. It is a wonderful thing to sow the seed and see the fullness of the harvest. Occasionally we are allowed to see it happen. Consecrated parents do often live to see the dreams and desires that they have had for their children come true; teachers occasionally see that those whom they once taught have learned so well the lessons which they sought to instill, that now and then a pupil has incorporated into his life some of the lessons that the teacher has advocated. For that to happen is the great compensation for being a teacher or a leader of youth.

No, the harvest that we reap is not only in our own lives, but in the lives of those about us. No man lives unto himself; all along the journey of life, whether consciously or unconsciously, we have been sowing seeds into the hearts and lives of those whose lives ours have touched. How vital it is that we scatter only good seed! To reap the whirlwind of our own misdeeds is tragic, but to have been the cause of evil in the lives of others is one of the saddest things on earth. Therefore, should all of us not strive daily to live in such a way that the result of our sowing may be a rich harvest and a glorious gathering of the sheaves when the final autumn crops are garnered?

> Season of mists and mellow fruitfulness,
>   Close bosom-friend of the maturing sun;
> Conspiring with him how to load and bless
>   With fruit the vines that round the thatch-eaves run;
> To bend with apples the moss'd cottage-trees,
>   And fill all fruit with ripeness to the core;
>   To swell the gourd, and plump the hazel shells
> With a sweet kernel; to set budding more,
>   And still more, later flowers for the bees,
>   Until they think warm days will never cease,
>   For Summer has o'er-brimm'd their clammy cells.[2]

[2] John Keats, "To Autumn," stanza 1

Chapter XV

SUMMER AND WINTER

❖❖

> "To-night the winds begin to rise
> And roar from yonder dropping day;
> The last red leaf is whirl'd away,
> The rooks are blown about the skies."
> —*Alfred Lord Tennyson*

> "Now learn a parable of the fig tree; When his branch is yet tender and putteth forth leaves, ye know that summer is nigh."
> —*Matt. 24:32*

*T*he certainty of God's laws is one of the comforting things in this uncertain world. We sometimes complain about these very certainties, especially when we have broken a law and must pay a penalty which irrevocably results. Yet this very inevitability is a protection. If the law were sometimes fulfilled and sometimes neglected, confusion and injustice would be the results. We then might well ask why one should be punished when someone else who is guilty of the same infraction goes scot-free. And as justice is administered with certainty, so are mercy, love, and other beautiful attributes of life. If we cast our bread on the waters, it is certain to come back to us, although we do not always recognize the manner of its return. There are many evidences of God's mercy and justice that we cannot understand now; for God's ways are not our ways, and in our short lives we cannot see his whole plan.

The same law of certainty applies both to the natural world and to the moral world. In spite of unexpected storms and other catastrophes of nature, ours is an orderly universe. God set the worlds and all the suns and stars in order at the time of creation, and he has never changed his laws. So we come again to the words in Genesis, "Summer and winter, and day and night shall not cease." Winter sometimes seems to linger on into "the lap of May," yet summer has never failed to come. Heat may plague us long after the calendar announces that autumn has come, and Indian summer warmth may prevail until after the Christmas season, but one morning we are sure to awake to find a snow-covered world—and it is winter.

Thomas Campion wrote:

> The summer hath his joys,
> And winter his delights.

Summer is a time of greater relaxation; a time more conducive to playing than working. It is a time of gaily-blooming flowers, trees heavily laden with fragrant, ripened fruit, and of stretches of shady, grassy fields tempting us to waste hours resting in lazy idleness in their cool lushness. In winter the flowers are dead, the fruit trees are barren, and the bleak fields are frozen wastes or snow-covered deserts. Only the sturdiest linger out-of-doors; most of us seek the warm indoors, and welcome any chance to dream before an open fire. Yet winter has its delights as well as summer, and cold sparkling winter days can send us to our tasks with a zest for getting things done such as we feel in no other kind of weather. God was good when he provided for us the variety of seasons, each with its own particular use in the plan of life.

Each season has its own beauty. Summer spreads out a panorama of richly varied colors against a background of so many shades of green that a painter has difficulty mixing his colors to catch every hue. Green-clad mountains lift their peaks into the azure of a summer sky; singing streams flow freely toward the sea, watering the thirsty land. Winter, on the other hand, brings the clean, clear-cut beauty of bare trees outlined against the sky, or the sparkle and gleam of a million diamonds in an ice-encrusted world. Snow may transform an ugly scene into a fairyland of pure, dazzling white with every tree, shrub, and small building changed into statues and shrines carved by a master architect. One must be dull of soul indeed not to be moved by such beauty, not to recognize the Creator who fashioned it, and to worship him, the Maker of all lovely things in the world.

Summer is the time for storing up the bountiful supply of food God provides; winter is the time to enjoy the results of the summer's industry. Summer is the season of youth and pleasure; winter is a time for age and quiet rest before an open fire. Is it not possible to see in these symbols a lesson in life? In the summertime of life we have zeal, vigor, and daring; there are no obstacles that one cannot overcome; no task is insurmountable. Let the Christian church enlist all the world's youth with these qualities of enthusiasm and ardor for God and his work, and the world can be won for him in one generation. Nothing is impossible to a determined, enthusiastic young man or woman. Is it not largely the fault of us who are older and have in our hands the guidance of youth if they fail to catch the vision and keep the torch of his love burning bright and lifted high to shed its light on all the world? Then when the winter season sets in and the evening of life has come we shall be ready for rest—

We shall rest, and, faith, we shall need it—lie down for an aeon or two,
Till the Master of All Good Workmen shall set us to work anew.[1]

"Summer and winter, seedtime and harvest. . . ." Our all-wise Father who has fixed the seasons in their places, has given us the freedom and power to arrange our lives in a pattern as perfectly designed for the fulfillment of the rich possibilities in our lives as he has fulfilled his dream of the infinite natural world. "O Lord, how manifold are thy works! in wisdom hast thou made them all: the earth is full of thy riches." (Ps. 104:24.)

[1] "When Earth's Last Picture is Painted." From: *The Seven Seas*, by Rudyard Kipling. Reprinted by permission of Mrs. George Bambridge, Doubleday & Company, Inc., and A. P. Watt & Son.

H. Armstrong Roberts

Chapter XVI

MORNING

❖❖

"And God said, Let there be light:
and there was light. And God saw the
light, that it was good: and God divided
the light from the darkness. And God
called the light Day, and the darkness
he called Night. And the evening and
the morning were the first day."

—Gen. 1:3-5

"When the morning stars sang together, and all the sons of God shouted
for joy."

—Job 38:7

To read thoughtfully and reverently the story of the Creation in the
first chapter of Genesis is to bring our finite spirits a little closer to the
infinite heart of God. What deep emotion the Creator must have experienced as, in response to his command, "Let there be light," he saw
the darkness roll back and the first dawn burst forth. As "evening and
morning were the first day," the glory of this dream's achievement
found expression in the simple yet deeply profound words, "And
God saw that it was good." Although during our own brief life span
we have seen the birth of thousands of days, it is difficult for us to imagine that first morning of creation. Yet we are able to see dawn drive
back the darkness and clothe the sky in rose, gray, and gold; and to behold the first rays of golden light illumine the earth as the sun rises
above the horizon.

Morning is a wonderful time. Shakespeare said, "Full many a glorious
morning have I seen." It is as if the world came every morning freshly
created from the hand of God. Sometimes the sun rises gloriously, bath-

ing the world in shining splendor; sometimes the sky is a gray curtain veiling the sun, so that the light is dim and obscured, and belief in its existence behind the clouds is an act of faith. The morning of a new day should bring to our hearts such joy as it brought to the heart of the little millgirl who sang as she went out into the morning of her one holiday in the whole year:

> The year's at the spring
> And day's at the morn;
> Morning's at seven;
> The hillside's dew-pearled;
> The lark's on the wing;
> The snail's on the thorn:
> God's in his heaven—
> All's right with the world!

Morning is a time of beginning again. How marvelous it is that each morning we may have a fresh page upon which to write the deeds of that day. It is our own fault if we carry over to the new page a smudged, unclean record and the careless or intentional mistakes of the preceding day. There may have been blank spaces left because of deeds of kindness left undone, but on the new page we may have an opportunity to leave no such blanks. It is a clean page; it is for us to fill with only clean thoughts, kind words, friendly deeds of sympathy and love, and to write into the record the fulfillment of at least some part of our life's great dream.

Morning should be a time of prayer, praise, and thanksgiving. God has brought us safely through a night of darkness and, perhaps even, of unseen dangers. We should certainly pause at the beginning of the day to thank him for his protection, for rest, and sleep. We should stand before him and ask for his guidance in all the affairs of the new day, and for strength to meet whatever trials and temptations may assail us. One of the loveliest scenes in *Paradise Lost* is the morning following a night during which Satan, in the shape of a toad, had squatted beside the ear of Eve and disturbed her sleep with whispers that caused her to have uneasy dreams. When she awoke beset by strange fears, Adam comforted his lovely spouse and gave her happy reassurance. Then, still pure and sinless, they stood together in the dawn of the most glorious day they had ever seen. There at the door of their bower, they lifted up

their souls in thanks and adoration to their Creator. Adam began his
prayer:

> These are thy glorious works, Parent of good,
> Almighty! thine this universal frame,
> Thus wondrous fair. Thyself how wondrous then!

and in such words as Milton only perhaps could imagine, Adam continued reverently to pour out thanks for all the marvelous works of
creation which God had showered upon them. Afterward they "firm
peace recovered soon, and wonted calm," and went forth amid dewy
flowers to pursue their accustomed tasks in the garden. Such a scene re-
minds us of the words of Job: "The morning stars sang together, and
all the sons of God shouted for joy."

The manner in which we spend the first minutes of the morning goes
a long way toward controlling our day. Norman Vincent Peale in *The
Power of Positive Thinking* urges that we lie quietly for a little while
after waking, repeating sentences and verses from God's Word and
breathing silent prayers of thanksgiving for his mercy and protection
through the night, and praying for guidance through the day. In *God's
Psychiatry* the author, C. L. Allen, suggests among other helpful passages of scripture, the thoughtful reading or recitation of the twenty-
third Psalm as one of the most effective preparations for meeting the day
with a serene and peaceful soul. If we practice this plan faithfully and
conscientiously, we may be surprised at how God will enable us to face
and conquer many situations that arise during the day. We will find that
the entire day goes better because of the therapy of thoughts of God and
communion with his spirit.

Morning is a time of preparation. In Ecclesiastes we read, "In the morning sow thy seed, and in the evening withhold not thine hand" (11:6).
Morning is representative of childhood and youth as times of preparation for the later years of life. Milton said:

> The childhood shows the man,
> As morning shows the day.

In "The Ode on the Intimations of Immortality," Wordsworth gives us
an immortal picture of the divine origin of life and God's guidance
through the years of youth to maturity, when man takes his place in
the world of labor for the Master:

95

Not in entire forgetfulness,
And not in utter nakedness,
But trailing clouds of glory do we come
From God, who is our home.
Heaven lies about us in our infancy;
Shades of the prison-house begin to close
Upon the growing boy,
But he beholds the light, and whence it flows.
He sees it in his joy;
The youth, who daily farther from the east
Must travel, still is Nature's priest,
And by the vision splendid
Is on his way attended;
At length the man perceives it die away,
And fade into the light of common day.

Morning! Let us thank God for the beginning of a new day—a day in which to live, to laugh, to sing, to work, to shed about us some of the marvelous sunshine of God's love and goodness. Let us raise our voices with Isaac Watts in words which he adapted from the Psalms:

Lord in the morning thou shalt hear
My voice ascending high.

H. Armstrong Roberts

Chapter XVII

EVENING

>"Evening, and morning, and at noon,
>will I pray, and cry aloud: and he shall
>hear my voice."
>
>*—Ps. 55:17*

>"Soon as the evening shades prevail,
>The moon takes up the wondrous tale."
>
>*—Addison*

Be the day weary or be the day long,
At length it draweth to even song.

E*vening* is a blessed time! Regardless of how the day has gone, we rejoice when evening comes. If it has been long, hard, or sad, we greet the evening with a sigh of relief for the close of the day, the coming of rest, and the blessed forgetfulness of sleep. If, on the other hand, the day has been full of joy and gladness, we may feel regretful because it is coming to an end; but evening brings with it a feeling of satisfaction and a song of praise for the gladness which God has let us enjoy. The calm and serenity that it brings are like a solemn benediction at the close of a beautiful service of worship.

Evening is a time for companionship with those we love. The very atmosphere of the hour of the day calls us together. It is a friendly time. At eventide we long most for those who are akin to us in spirit, those with whom we can speak of serious things—the things closest to our hearts. The two men who walked to Emmaus on that first Easter Sunday evening were near to each other in thought and spirit. Their love for the crucified Christ, their grief and amazement at all the events of the preceding days had drawn them close to each other. The evening was calm and peaceful after the storms and earthquakes of the past three days. The two men were on their way home, and their conversation was about the crucifixion. Hence they were prepared for him to join them and reveal to them that of which they had heard only rumors —that the crucified Lord had become the risen Saviour. We are told that their hearts burned within them as he talked; they were able to receive his message because their souls were tuned to him. Milton in giving us our first picture of Adam and Eve in the garden of Eden shows us another evening of beauty and peace. The purity and innocence of that sinless pair are reflected in the quiet evening, the gently cooling zephyrs, the flowery banks, the playful beasts, and the preparation of delectable fruits for supper. As a climax to the scene Milton wrote:

> for the sun,
> Declined, was hastening now with prone career
> To the Ocean Isles, and in the ascending scale
> Of Heaven the stars that usher evening rose.

What bliss was present here! How tragic it was that Satan was even then nearby plotting the downfall of this perfect pair!

Evening is the children's hour. The time between the daylight and dark offers many delights. Do you remember the pleasure of being allowed to go out after supper in long summer twilights to play with neighborhood children until darkness began to fall and your mother's call brought you home? It is one of the happy memories of my childhood. Twilight was also a perfect time for storytelling. When the light had faded too much to read, and it was not yet dark enough to light the lamps, what fun it was to curl up on the sofa or in a big chair and listen to favorite childhood stories. We read and hear much today of the lack of security and love in childhood as one of the prime causes of juvenile delinquency. Could anything give a child a safer feeling and surer knowledge of being loved and wanted than such evenings as these?

The psalmist said: "Man goeth forth unto his work and to his labour until the evening" (104:23). "The Cotter's Saturday Night" is the finest picture in literature of a simple, honest, God-fearing father as he sets aside the tools with which he has toiled all week, and goes home from the fields to gather his family around him for an evening of companionship and strengthening of family ties. The boys and girls in service in the neighborhood come home; and accompanying Jenny, the eldest, is her young man, who, by his manly appearance and modest demeanor, wins the approval of her parents. What nostalgic feelings Burns creates as he tells of the events of the evening—the simple evening meal, using the best china and a very special homemade cheese saved—all brought out to please Jenny and to honor her friend; after supper the father's reverent reading of the Bible, and simple prayers of praise and faith uttered by various members of the family; group singing of well-known hymns and beloved folk songs; and with it all such friendly talk and joking as only a close-knit family can engage in.

Such scenes as this in homes around the world would defeat communism and go a long way toward putting an end to the horrible crimes that terrorize people and threaten the very continuation of civilization.

Evening is a time for contemplation. How great is the world's present need for peace and quiet! So few people take time to go apart and commune with their own souls. It seems that not enough people have sufficient concern with the realities of life to have anything important to talk over with themselves. Such a period for them would be a barren hour. But increasingly the greatest leaders in every area of life—science, education, economics, religion—are coming to the definite conclusion that the turmoil, confusion, and disorder in the world cannot be corrected, and peace established among nations, until individuals find greater peace within their own souls. Never have there been so many books written and so many sermons preached on ways to bring peace and serenity into one's own mind and heart. I believe that if everybody would set aside an hour a day for contemplation and prayer, much of the disorder could be cured; and there would come the revival of religion which is now recognized by everyone as the only way by which the world can be saved. We need to follow the advice of the Scriptures: "Be still, and know that I am God."

The evening of life is a beautiful symbol of old age. Browning says that old age is the best of life: "The last of life for which the first was made." The picture he paints is old age as it should be, and is, unfortunately, not true of everyone who grows old. The struggles, hardships, and trials of making a living, of supporting a family, of arriving at a goal are past; and one is ready for rest. Just as we often see a glorious sunset ushering in a peaceful evening, at the end of a stormy, tempestuous day, so may be the closing days of life. Sunset is the opening of the gate into eternal life, the glorious fulfillment of God's plan for us.

During his eightieth year Tennyson wrote his last poem one of the best-known and best-loved poems in the world—beloved by those who are themselves approaching the shores of that vast sea and by those whose loved ones have already crossed over to the other side. All of us know it.

Sunset and evening Star,
   And one clear call for me!
And may there be no moaning of the bar,
   When I put out to sea,

But such a tide as moving seems asleep,
   Too full for sound and foam,
When that which drew from out the boundless deep
   Turns again home.

Twilight and evening bell,
   And after that the dark!
And may there be no sadness of farewell,
   When I embark;

For tho' from out our bourne of Time and Place
   The flood may bear me far,
I hope to see my Pilot face to face
   When I have crossed the bar.

H. Armstrong Roberts

Chapter XVIII

NIGHT

❖❖

> "Day unto day uttereth speech, and night unto night sheweth knowledge."
> —*Ps. 19:2*

> "And it came to pass in those days, that he went out into a mountain to pray, and continued all night in prayer to God."
> —*Luke 6:12*

> "Praised be my Lord for our sister the Moon, and for the Stars, the which He has set clear and lovely in the heaven."
> —*Francis of Assisi*

O*ur* Father seems to delight in contrasts; they abound in the world of nature. After the cold of winter comes the heat of summer; clouds are always followed by sunshine; one may climb to the loftiest mountain peak, but a valley lies at its foot. As surely as the day dawns, night will follow, bringing darkness after sunlight, peace and quiet after the confusion and noise of the day, and sweet, refreshing rest after toil.

The world has for so long associated darkness with ignorance and sin that we are prone to forget that it has its blessings as well. The moon and stars are as certainly in the heavens during the hours of daylight as during the night, but the brightness of the sun obscures them. We should miss some of God's greatest gifts of beauty if darkness did not reveal the moon and stars to us. Shakespeare wrote of the "blessed candles of the night," and in his great hymn Addison said:

> Soon as the evening shades prevail,
> The moon takes up the wondrous tale,

> And nightly to the listening Earth
> Repeats the story of her birth.

Our eyes often grow weary from the brightness and glare of a brilliant, sunshiny day, and we welcome the soothing comfort of darkness. As we rest in the darkness, our thoughts often turn inward. Night is a time for study and meditation. Milton made night hours the setting for "Il Penseroso," the mood of the thoughtful man. Night and darkness can shut out the noise and distractions of the outside world, and turn our thoughts toward God. Christ used the night hours for his personal and intimate prayers and his communion with his Father. Before choosing his disciples, those twelve men who were to carry on his plans for the salvation of the world, "He went out into a mountain to pray, and continued all night in prayer to God" (Luke 6:12). As Christ's ministry drew to its close, Luke tells us, "And in the day time he was teaching in the temple; and at night he went out, and abode in the mount that is called the mount of Olives" (21:37). If Christ, Son of God, needed communion with his Father at all the critical times in his ministry, how much more should we seek to learn his will and hear his voice!

How many great, important decisions and choices have been made by his followers after long hours of prayer in the silent watches of the night in all the centuries since Christ walked on the earth. There is no time during the twenty-four hours of our day when we can be so withdrawn from the world, or feel more certainly the presence of God as in the solitary darkness, alone with our Creator. It is the best time for us to pour out our needs and our problems, and listen quietly while he talks to us. The words of the psalmist are true: "Day unto day uttereth speech, and night unto night sheweth knowledge" (19:2).

Just as night is the most suitable time for prayer, it is also the most fruitful time for study. It is well known that alone Edison often continued his experiments throughout the entire night, working zealously to complete some experiment that demanded his undivided attention and undisturbed continuity. His experience has been duplicated by many men and women who have succeeded far better than the less ambitious and those less zealous to attain success. Milton expressed such ambition as this in lines from "Il Penseroso":

> Or let my lamp, at midnight hour,
> Be seen in some high lonely tower,
> Where I may oft outwatch the bear.

From childhood some of us may have quoted the well-known lines, which convey a far deeper truth than we realize—lines from Longfellow's "Ladder of St. Augustine":

> The heights by great men reached and kept
> Were not attained by sudden flight,
> But they, while their companions slept,
> Were toiling upward in the night.

Night is the time for sleeping. In Ecclesiastes we read, "The sleep of a labouring man is sweet" (5:12). When one has spent a long day in exhausting labor, how welcome is the night with its promise of rest and sleep: "Sleep that knits up the ravell'd sleave of care." A mother, who has cared for her small child through the long day, looks with tender love upon the child asleep in his crib, and rejoices in the hours of rest ahead. A sick person, tired from a long day of pain and suffering, welcomes night when, soothed and tended by a skillful nurse, he may lie in the friendly darkness and fall into restful sleep. All of us experience days that bring burdens and trials lengthening the hours and trying our souls; then God gives to us a night of restful sleep, and we wake in the morning refreshed and ready for the tasks that the day may bring. We wake with the words on our lips, "Thank God for night and sleep!"

In "Night Thoughts" Edward Young wrote: "By night an atheist half believes in a God." How can anyone stand under a starlit sky or see the clear-cut shadows and light cast by a full moon and not wholly believe that only a Father who loved his children completely would create such beauty for them?

The peace and rest which night brings are another evidence of God's care for us. The psalmist said, "I will both lay me down in peace, and sleep" (1:8), and, "He giveth his beloved sleep" (127:2).

So to God, the giver of every good and perfect gift, we raise our hymn of praise for the beauty of the night, its comforting darkness, its blessed rest and sleep, and for its hours best-suited to meditation and communion with him.

> How beautiful is night!
> A dewy freshness fills the silent air:
> In full-orbed glory yonder moon divine
> Rolls through the dark blue depths.[1]

[1] Robert Southey, "Thalaba," bk. I, st. 1.

Chapter XIX

GOD'S WORLD

❖❖

"The Lord reigneth, he is clothed
with majesty; the Lord is clothed with
strength, wherewith he hath girded himself: the world also is stablished, that it
cannot be moved."

—Ps. 93:1

"This is my Father's world,
And to my listening ears,
All nature sings, and 'round me rings
The music of the spheres.
This is my Father's world:
I rest me in the thought
Of rocks and trees, of skies and seas;
His hand the wonders wrought.

"This is my Father's world,
The birds their carols raise,
The morning light, the lily white,
Declare their Maker's praise.
This is my Father's world:
He shines in all that's fair;
In the rustling grass I hear Him pass,
He speaks to me everywhere."

—Maltbie D. Babcock

Whether there are additional worlds where other human races dwell nobody can say for sure at this time; but we know certainly that we live in a world created by a great and loving Father who made it beautiful enough to be the home of his children—children made in his image and loved by him with "a love as high as heaven, as wide as the universe, and as lasting as eternity."

An earthly father builds for his children the best home he can afford; our heavenly Father, with all the resources of infinity at his command, gave to his children a world, lighted by the sun during the day, flooded with the silver light of the moon by night, and lying under the matchless beauty of the star-sown vault of the firmament. He piled up mountains, snow-covered or tree-clad; he spread out the oceans with a sunlit surf breaking gently on the beaches of the world, or with great waters rising in majestic, storm-tossed waves which move us to silence and awe. He clothed the land in a hundred tints of restful green, and adorned the earth with blossoming trees and flowers of a thousand hues and fragrances. He created birds of brilliant plumage and small birds with thrilling music in their throats; he fashioned animals, large and small, to roam the forests; he placed in the sea huge whales and small fish, some of whose colors rival the birds and flowers.

And it was our Father's pleasure to place man—a thinking, reasonable creature, with a soul capable of loving and worshiping the Creator, and the endowment of being able to live in harmony with the works of creation, and affection and neighborliness with other men—in dominion over all created things. If man would order his life in accord with God's law, wars would cease, men would live as brothers, and there would be the peace and good will which Christ came to bring to earth. His kingdom can come in the world only if we individually incorporate into our lives the principles which Christ taught and followed when he lived among men on earth.

It is we his creatures who have failed, not God. Seasons never fail; droughts may threaten, but rain finally comes; and beauty is renewed on every hand. God's world, as he planned it, is the home of man in preparation for the perfect home of eternity—that home beyond the stars, a home of such magnificence that Paul writing to the Corinthians said: "Eye hath not seen, nor ear heard, neither have entered into the heart of man, the things which God hath prepared for them that love him" (I Cor. 2:9).

The keynote and cornerstone of this world, and the foundation on which the world to come is built is love—such love as Christ taught throughout his ministry. It was this love which he held up before the lawyer when the lawyer asked him, "Master, which is the great commandment in the law?" (Matt. 22:36.)

And Christ answered, "Thou shalt love the Lord thy God with all

110

thy heart, and with all thy soul, and with all thy mind. And the second is like unto it, Thou shalt love thy neighbor as thyself." (Matt. 22:37, 39.)

In *The Brothers Karamazov*, Dostoyevsky gave a great picture of the power of love in the world.

Love all God's creation, the whole and every grain of sand in it. Love every leaf, every ray of God's light. Love the animals, love the plants, love everything. If you love everything, you will perceive the divine mystery in things. Once you perceive it, you will begin to comprehend it better every day. And you will come at last to love the whole world with an all-embracing love.

	DATE DUE		